MACMILLAN FIRST ILLUSTRATED DICTIONARY

MACMILLAN

© Copyright text R. Nesbitt 1990
© Copyright illustrations Macmillan Education Ltd 1993

All rights reserved. No reproduction, copy or transmission of this publication may be made without written permission.

No paragraph of this publication may be reproduced, copied or transmitted save with written permission or in accordance with the provisions of the Copyright, Designs and Patents Act 1988, or under the terms of any licence permitting limited copying issued by the Copyright Licensing Agency, 90 Tottenham Court Road, London W1P 9HE.

Any person who does any unauthorised act in relation to this publication may be liable to criminal prosecution and civil claims for damages.

First published 1990 by
MACMILLAN EDUCATION LTD
London and Basingstoke
Companies and representatives throughout the world

ISBN 0-333-55706-9

14	13	12	11	10	9	8	7	6
07	06	05	04	03	02	01	00	99

This book is printed on paper suitable for recycling and made from fully managed and sustained forest sources.

Printed in Malaysia

Cover design and illustrations by Mark de Lange

How to use the dictionary

All pupils in Primary should be encouraged to use this dictionary, either as a picture book to learn words and meanings, a first reader, or a simple dictionary.

Children should look at the pictures and read the words (once they have learnt to read in English). Encourage them to remember the words using both words and pictures, and then using pictures only. Allow them to draw pictures from the words.

Encourage the children to read the example sentences, and to produce whole example sentences of their own.

Help the children to use the information to build ideas and sentences, and increasingly, to use the book as a dictionary.

Let the children use the book as often as possible: apart from developing basic dictionary skills, they will develop reading and sentence construction skills.

Talking about people and things:

Words like I, he, them, your, and so on are hard to explain clearly. (These words do *not* appear as separate entries in the dictionary.) In order to learn to use them quickly and easily, look at the table below. Teachers should use this table to help the children understand how these words are used.

When I talk about myself (me), I say

| I like chocolate. | David likes **me**. | That is **my** book. | That is **mine**. |

When I talk to someone, I say

| **You** are tall. | David likes **you**. | That is **your** book. | That is **yours**. |

When I talk about a boy or a man, I say

| **He** is tall. | David likes **him**. | That is **his** book. | That is **his**. |

When I talk about a girl or a woman, I say

| **She** is pretty. | David likes **her**. | That is **her** book. | That is **hers**. |

When I talk about a thing or an animal, I say

| **It** is beautiful. | David likes **it**. | That is **its** tail. |

When I talk about myself and other people, I say

| **We** are happy. | David likes **us**. | That is **our** car. | That is **ours**. |

When I talk about a lot of people or a lot of things, I say

| **They** are big. | David likes **them**. | That is **their** car. | That is **theirs**. |

There are many examples of these words in the dictionary. Make sure the children practise using them properly.

A a B b C c D d E e F f G g H h I i J j K k L l M m

Aa

a one
John is reading a book.

able to can do something
My sister is able to swim.

about 1 almost, nearly
His brother is about ten years old.
    2 to do with
He told me a story about a hare.

above higher than
She has a clock above her bed.

absent not here
My sister is absent from school. She is ill.

accept take something a person gives you
I accept your invitation to the party.

accident something bad that happens
The old lady was hurt in the car accident.

ache a pain which hurts for a long time
Mother had a headache all morning.

across from one side to the other
They built a bridge across the river.

act 1 be in a play
My brother is going to act in the school play.
    2 do something
You must act quickly to save his life.

6

N n O o P p Q q R r S s T t U u V v W w X x Y y Z z

add find the answer to a sum
What do you get if you add four and three?

4 + 3 = 7

address the place where you live
My address   1 Main St.

adult a grown-up person
My mother and father are adults.

adventure something exciting that you do
Going to the country was a great adventure.

advertisement a picture to show people things to buy
I saw an advertisement for bicycles in the window.

aeroplane a machine for flying
Aeroplanes carry people around the world.

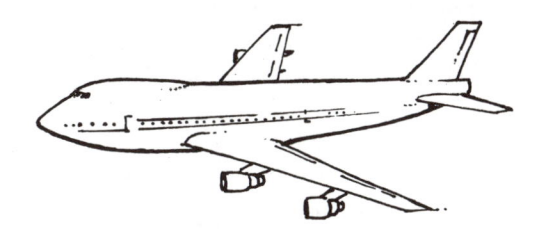

afraid feel fear
I am afraid of snakes and spiders.

after 1 behind
The lion's tail comes after its head and body.
      2 later
I will see you after tea.

afternoon from twelve noon until about five o'clock
School finishes at about three o'clock in the afternoon.

again once more
Do not do it again.

age how old you are
Are you twelve years of age?

ago in the past
Dinosaurs lived millions of years ago.

7

A a B b C c D d E e F f G g H h I i J j K k L l M m

agree say yes
I agree to go to the party with you.

aim point a gun
He aimed his gun at the antelope.

air the gases we breathe every day
We need to breathe air to live.

airport a place where aeroplanes arrive and leave
My father is flying from Nairobi. I am going to the airport to meet him.

alight on fire
The paper and the twigs kept the fire alight.

alive living
Will you be alive in A.D. 2010?

all everyone or everything
All the elephants in the park are dead.

almost nearly
Look! It is almost four o'clock.

alone by yourself
I was alone in the empty house.

N n O o P p Q q R r S s T t U u V v W w X x Y y Z z

along from one end to the other
He ran along the path to the house.

aloud in a voice you can hear
I want you to say the poem aloud.

alphabet all the letters in a language
A is the first letter of the alphabet.

altogether counting everyone or everything
There are forty pupils in the class altogether.

always all the time
The sun always sets in the west.

ambulance a van to take sick people to hospital
They put the lady with the broken leg in the ambulance.

among to be with other people or things
I found some paper among my school books.

amuse make someone laugh
The clown amused the children at the party.

anchor a large metal hook, it keeps a ship in one place
The ship stopped and dropped its anchor.

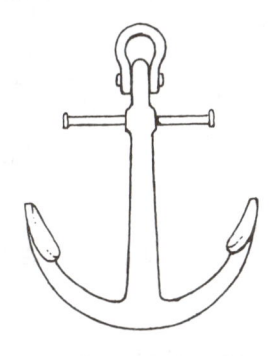

angel a messenger from God
The angel brought the news to the shepherds.

angle the corner where two lines meet
How big are the angles in that triangle?

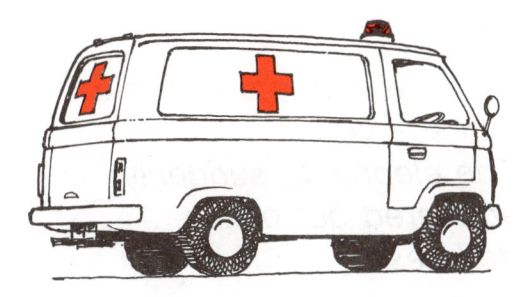

9

A a B b C c D d E e F f G g H h I i J j K k L l M m

angry cross
Mother was very angry. I broke two plates.

animal living things which can move
Dogs, horses and men are all types of animals.

ankle the joint between your foot and your leg
My brother hurt his ankle.

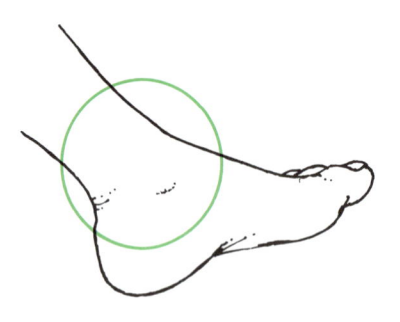

another one more
You cannot have another biscuit.

ant a tiny insect
Millions of ants live together in an anthill.

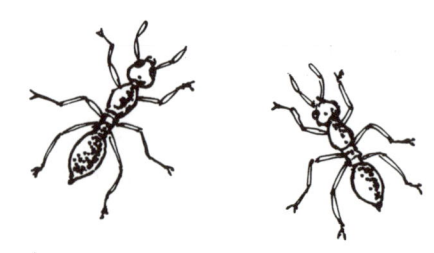

antelope an African deer
There are antelopes in many parts of Africa.

anybody or **anyone** any person at all
Can anyone lend me a pencil?

anywhere any place
I cannot find my coat anywhere.

appear come so people can see you
The elephants suddenly appeared out of the darkness.

N n O o P p Q q R r S s T t U u V v W w X x Y y Z z

apple a round red or green juicy fruit
There are some apples on the plate.

approach come near
It is dangerous to approach wild animals.

April the fourth month of the year
April comes after March.

apron a cloth worn over your clothes to keep them clean
Mother always wears an apron when she is cooking.

are part of verb 'to be' – we are, you are, they are
We are happy. They are sad.

arithmetic working with numbers
You can add, divide and multiply in arithmetic.

ark a kind of boat
The ark saved Noah and his family from the flood.

arm the part of the body from the shoulder to the hand.
Use both arms to pick up the box.

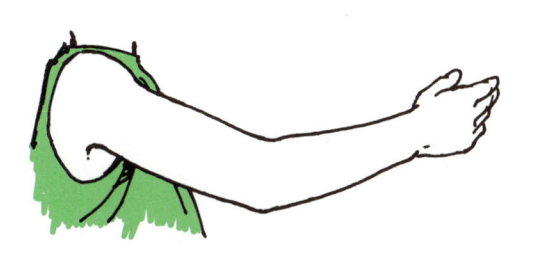

11

A a B b C c D d E e F f G g H h I i J j K k L l M m

army a lot of people trained to fight on the ground
Soldiers in the army use tanks and guns and rifles.

around all round
The road ran around the town.

arrive come to the end of a journey
We hope to arrive home at eight o'clock.

arrow a sharp stick you shoot from a bow
The hunter shot the antelope with a poisoned arrow.

artist a person who draws or paints pictures
The artist painted a picture of the lake.

ash the grey powder left after something burns
The wind blew the ash from the fire all over the house.

asleep sleeping
The cat was asleep in front of the fire.

assembly when the whole school meets together
We sing a song at morning assembly.

12

N n O o P p Q q R r S s T t U u V v W w X x Y y Z z

astronaut a person who travels in space
Two American astronauts landed on the moon.

athlete a person who runs or jumps for sport
My brother is an athlete who enjoys running.

atlas a book of maps
An atlas helps you to learn the countries of the world.

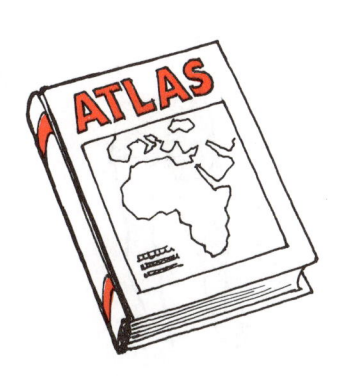

August the eighth month of the year
September comes after August.

aunt the sister of your father or mother, or your uncle's wife
My aunt gives me money on my birthday.

author a person who writes books
I do not know the author of this book.

autumn the part of the year after summer
It is beautiful in Lesotho in autumn.

awake not asleep
I was awake all night with a headache.

away the distance to another place
My uncle's house is five kilometres away.

axe a tool for chopping wood
You need a sharp axe for cutting wood.

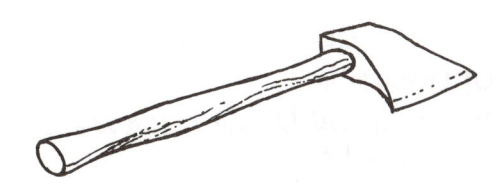

13

A a **B b** C c D d E e F f G g H h I i J j K k L l M m

Bb

baby a very young child
The baby was crying for its milk.

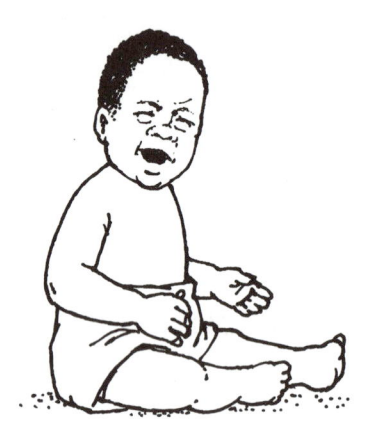

back the part of your body from your neck to your bottom
The baby monkey climbed onto its mother's back.

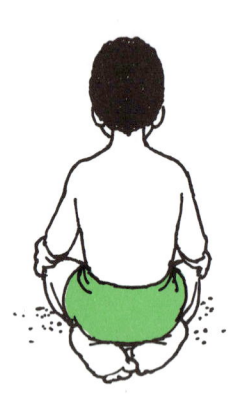

backwards going the opposite way
If you spell DAM backwards you get MAD.

bad naughty, not good
He is a bad man. He stole a chicken.

bag a paper, cloth or plastic sack to carry things in
He had a bag of apples and a bag of bananas.

bake cook in an oven
Mother is baking a cake for my birthday.

balance keep something steady
The boy was balancing the ball on his head.

14

N n O o P p Q q R r S s T t U u V v W w X x Y y Z z

bald without any hair
My old uncle is bald. He has no hair on his head.

banana a long fruit with a yellow skin
The boy ate a banana for lunch.

ball a round object. You can kick or throw it
They were playing with their new ball.

balloon a small rubber bag filled with air
The boy blew up the green balloon.

band 1 a long piece of material put around something
Mother's hat had a green band around it.

2 a group of people who play music together
The band played and the children danced.

15

A a **B b** C c D d E e F f G g H h I i J j K k L l M m

bandage a piece of cloth tied around a cut
The doctor put a bandage around the boy's leg.

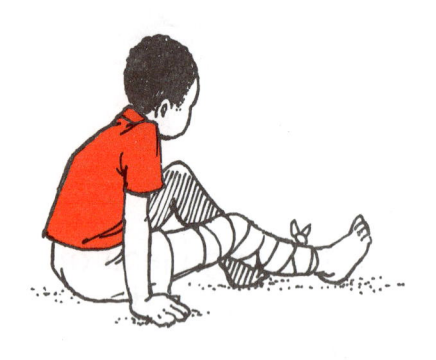

bang a loud noise
The door closed with a bang.

bank 1 the ground at the side of a river
We watched the fish from the bank of the river.

2 a place where people keep their money
I put my money in the bank every week.

bar a rod made of wood or metal
The bars on the lion's cage are very thick.

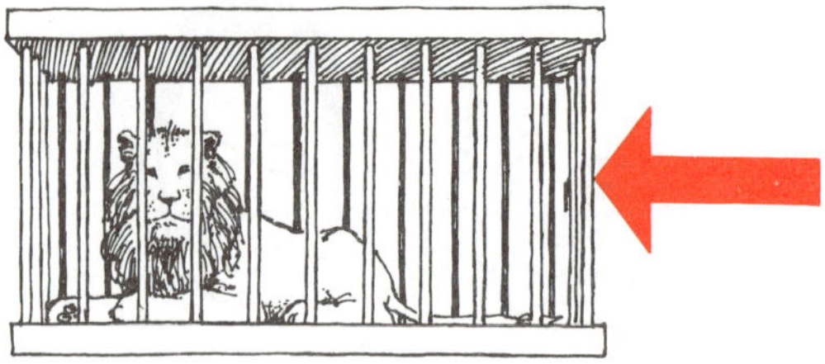

bare not wearing any clothes
The boy was bare to his waist.

bark 1 the sound a dog makes
The dog barked at the birds in the tree.
2 the outside cover of a tree
The tree had a smooth bark.

barrel a round container with flat ends
The barrel was full of beer.

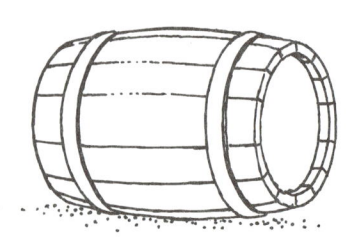

N n O o P p Q q R r S s T t U u V v W w X x Y y Z z

basin a big, deep bowl to hold water
She washed the plates in the basin.

basket a bag made of straw or thin wood
There are seven eggs in the basket.

bat 1 a small mouse-like animal with wings
Bats like to fly at night.

2 a thick stick for hitting a ball
I throw the ball and you hit it with the bat.

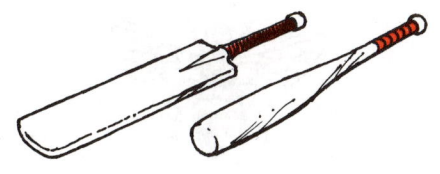

bath a big basin. You sit in it to wash all over
He told the dirty boy to get into the bath.

battery electricity in a small tube. You put the tube in a torch or radio
My father put a new battery in his torch.

be part of the verb 'to be'
I want to be a nurse when I leave school.

beak the hard part of a bird's mouth
The eagle was holding a fish in its beak.

17

A a **B b** C c D d E e F f G g H h I i J j K k L l M m

bean a long, green vegetable with big seeds
Mother cooked the beans for supper.

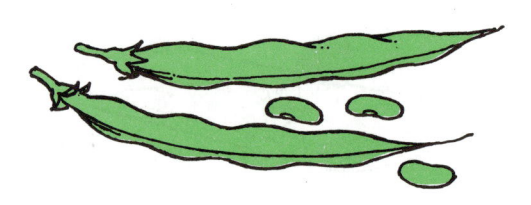

bear a large animal with sharp claws and thick fur
The bear's thick coat keeps it warm in winter.

beard the hair that grows on a man's chin
The old man had a long beard.

beast a large animal
We heard the cry of a wild beast from the woods.

beat 1 hit with a stick many times
The man beat the boy with a stick.
2 come first, win
The teachers always beat the pupils at football.

beautiful lovely to look at or listen to
She was very beautiful. She had dark hair and dark eyes.

because telling the reason
I ran home because it was going to rain.

bed the thing you sleep on
Lie on the bed and go to sleep.

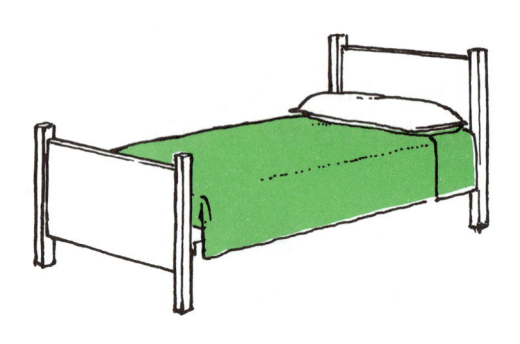

bee a small insect that makes honey
The bees are in that tree.

18

N n O o P p Q q R r S s T t U u V v W w X x Y y Z z

beef the meat from cows and bulls
The beef was cut up to make a stew.

beer a strong drink
Uncle buys his beer from the bottle store.

beetle an insect with hard covers on its wings
The green beetle had black spots on its back.

bell a metal object that rings when it is hit
The teacher rang the school bell.

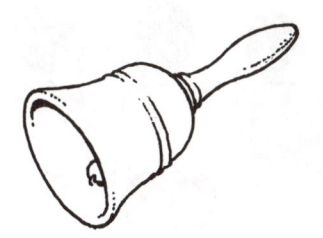

belong 1 owned by someone
That pencil belongs to me.
2 part of
Do you belong to the football team?

below under
The snake slid below the stone.

belt a band you wear around your waist
Sarah wore a green belt round her dress.

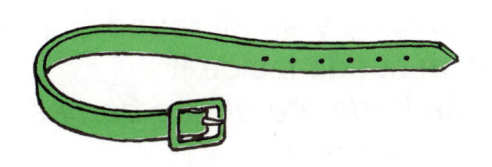

before earlier than
The cows came home before the goats.

begin start
Mother asked me to begin to dig the garden.

behind at the back of
The puppy hid behind its mother.

19

A a **B b** C c D d E e F f G g H h I i J j K k L l M m

bench a wooden or stone seat for more than one person
The three boys sat on the bench.

bend a turn in the road
The bus drove round the bend too fast.

beneath under
The boat sailed beneath the bridge.

berry any small round fruit with seeds inside it
The birds ate all the berries off the bush.

beside at the side of, next to
The dog was sitting beside the cat.

best better than all the others
He is the best footballer in the class.

better more than good
Maria's cake is better than Sarah's.

between in the middle
The boy sat between his mother and his father.

beyond further than
The spaceship is going beyond the moon.

Bible the holy book of the Christians
John reads the Bible every night.

bicycle a machine with two wheels and pedals. You can ride on it
David rides his bicycle to school every day.

N n O o P p Q q R r S s T t U u V v W w X x Y y Z z

big large
The horse could not jump over the big wall.

bill a piece of paper. It tells you how much money you have to pay
John paid the bill for the chicken he bought.

bin a large container for rubbish or corn
Please put those old tins in the bin.

bird an animal with two legs, feathers, wings and a beak
The birds flew high into the sky.

birth the time you are born
The cat gave birth to five kittens.

biscuit a small, thin, dry cake
John had two biscuits with his tea.

bit a small piece
Maria only ate a small bit of the cake.

bite cut something with your teeth
She bit into the apple.

black very dark, no light
The night was black. There were no stars.

blanket a thick cover on a bed
In winter I need three blankets on my bed.

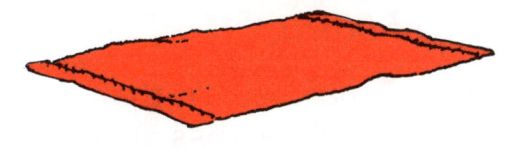

bleed lose blood
His nose began to bleed.

blind not able to see
The boy helped the blind man across the road.

21

A a **B b** C c D d E e F f G g H h I i J j K k L l M m

blink open and close your eyes very quickly
Mother blinked as she cut the onion.

blood the red liquid in your body
The girl cried when she saw blood on her finger.

blow 1 a hard hit
The boy fell after the first blow.
2 make air come out of your mouth quickly
I will blow out the candle.

blue the colour of the sky on a sunny day
Mother was wearing a blue hat.

blunt not sharp, cannot cut
The blunt knife would not cut the meat.

board a long flat piece of wood
Father made a shelf with a piece of board.

boat a small vehicle that carries people across water
The boat took them across the lake.

body all of a person or animal
The mouse had a fat little body.

boil 1 a sore spot on your skin
Sarah had a boil on her face.
2 heat a liquid until it bubbles
Father boiled the water for his tea.

bone the hard parts of an animal's body
John fell off the wall and broke a bone in his arm.

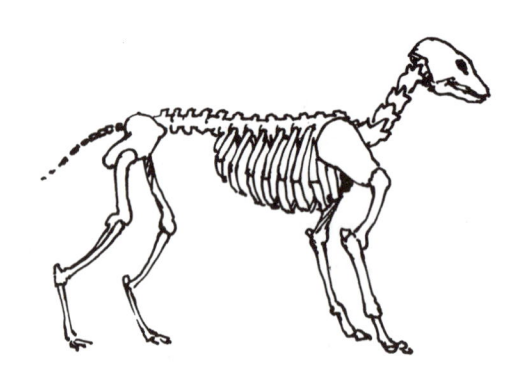

book sheets of paper fixed together in a cover
My father was reading a book about cars.

N n O o P p Q q R r S s T t U u V v W w X x Y y Z z

boot 1 a kind of shoe which covers the foot and ankle
He wears boots in the winter when it is cold.

2 the part of the car where you put bags and boxes
The girl put her case in the boot of the car.

both two things or two people
David ate both the bananas.

bottle a glass or plastic container for liquids
She bought two bottles of orange juice at the shop.

bottom 1 the lowest part of something
The fish lay on the bottom of the river.

2 the part of your body you sit on
John hurt his bottom when he fell off the chair.

born when a baby comes into the world
I was born on the fourth of March.

bounce spring up and down like a ball
The football bounced against the wall.

23

A a **B b** C c D d E e F f G g H h I i J j K k L l M m

bow 1 the wood and string for shooting an arrow
He put an arrow into his bow.

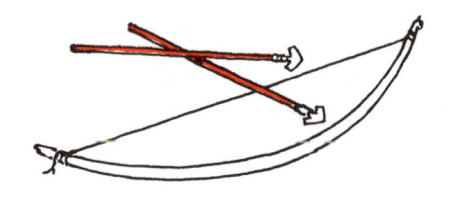

2 a kind of knot
Please tie the string in a bow.

bowl a round deep dish
Mother put the bowl of fruit on the table.

boy a male child
The boy climbed the tree.

brake a part of a vehicle. It stops it or slows it down
The man was unable to stop the car. The brakes were not working.

branch the part of the tree that grows out from the trunk
Many birds build their nests in the branches of trees.

brave not afraid of pain or danger
John was very brave. He helped the police to catch the thieves.

bread the food you make by baking a mixture of flour, water and yeast
Mary had bread and butter for lunch.

break make something go to pieces
When I break a glass, father is very angry.

N n O o P p Q q R r S s T t U u V v W w X x Y y Z z

breathe take air into your body through your mouth or nose
We cannot breathe under water.

breeze a soft, gentle wind
The breeze moved the leaves on the trees.

brick a block of hard clay or cement
They used red bricks to build the wall.

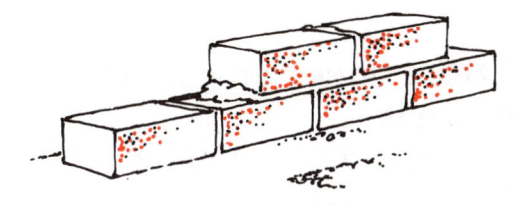

bride a woman who has just married
The bride wore a long white dress on her wedding day.

bridge a road built over a river or a railway
I watched the boats go under the bridge.

bright giving off a lot of light
The stars shone brightly in the dark sky.

bring come with or carry
Tom is bringing his friend to lunch on Saturday.

broad wide
The boat sailed across the broad river.

brooch a piece of jewellery pinned to a dress
She wore a red brooch on her dress.

broom a brush with a long handle for cleaning the floor
The children took brooms and started to clean the floor.

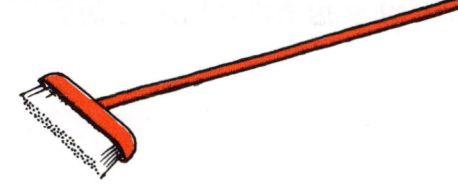

brother a boy in the family with other children
My brother is taller than I am.

brown the colour of chocolate or tea
Tea leaves in a tea-cup are dark brown.

25

A a **B b** C c D d E e F f G g H h I i J j K k L l M m

bruise a sore place on the skin
John fell off the chair. He bruised his arm.

brush a tool with short hairs to keep your hair neat. We also use it for cleaning or painting
I brush my hair every morning.

bubble a ball of air inside a liquid
My Coke is full of bubbles.

bucket a round container with a handle for carrying water
David filled his bucket at the well.

bud a flower or leaf before it opens
The caterpillar ate all the buds on the bush.

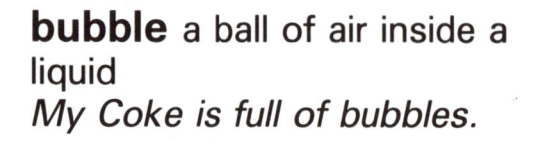

build make something by fitting pieces together
It took two years to build the house.

building a place to work in or live in
My father's office is in that building.

N n O o P p Q q R r S s T t U u V v W w X x Y y Z z

bull a male animal, male cattle
John's father has three bulls and thirty cows on his farm.

bullet a small piece of metal, it comes out of a gun
The bullet missed the antelope. It hit a tree.

bump a bruise on the skin
The baby had a large bump on her head where she fell.

bunch a number of things joined or tied together
She bought a bunch of flowers in the market.

burn set fire to or be on fire
The dry wood burned very quickly.

burst break open suddenly
The balloon burst in John's face.

bus a large vehicle to carry a lot of people
The children travel to school in the bus every day.

bush a small tree
The birds ate the berries on the bush.

busy having a lot to do
My father is busy in the garden.

butcher someone who sells meat
Joe bought a kilogram of meat from the butcher.

A a **B b** C c D d E e F f G g H h I i J j K k L l M m

butter a yellow food made from cream
I like to eat bread and butter.

butterfly an insect with big coloured wings
The butterfly had red and black wings.

button a small round thing on clothes, it goes through a hole to hold the clothes together
Mother sewed a button on to my shirt.

buy get something by paying money for it
My uncle is going to buy me a bicycle for my birthday.

buzzard a large hawk that kills and eats small animals
The buzzard carried the mouse back to its nest.

by 1 using
The cooker works by gas.
    2 not later than
We will be there by six o'clock.

Cc

cabbage a round vegetable with green leaves
I do not like cooked cabbage.

cactus a green desert plant, it is covered in sharp points like needles
A cactus needs very little water.

N n O o P p Q q R r S s T t U u V v W w X x Y y Z z

cafe a place where you can buy a drink or a meal
We stopped at the cafe for coffee and cakes.

cage a box with bars
The lion tried to escape from its cage.

cake a food made with flour, butter, eggs and sugar and baked in an oven
I had a chocolate cake for my birthday.

calendar a list of all the days, weeks and months in a year
Jane crossed off the days on her calendar.

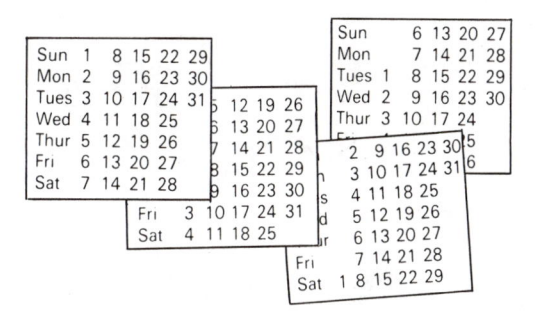

calf 1 a young cow or bull
The calf followed its mother.
2 the back part of the leg between the knee and the ankle
Jason ran the race with a bandage around his calf.

call 1 speak loudly
She called her sister's name when she saw her.
2 visit someone
She called to see her friend.
3 named
She is called Marie.

29

A a B b **C c** D d E e F f G g H h I i J j K k L l M m

camel a big animal with two humps on its back used for carrying people or things
Camels are used in very dry places. They can travel without much water.

can 1 a container, it is made of tin
Father needs three cans of oil for the car.
   2 able to do something
I can read and write.

camera a machine for taking photographs
The boy took a photograph of his mother with his new camera.

camp a place where people live in huts or tents for a short time
They stayed at the camp for a weekend.

canal a man-made river
The Suez Canal goes from the Mediterranean to the Red Sea.

N n O o P p Q q R r S s T t U u V v W w X x Y y Z z

candle a light made from a stick of wax with string through it. The string burns slowly
We lit the candles when the lights went out.

car a vehicle on four wheels with an engine, it carries people
Uncle Joe bought a new car last week.

caravan a small house on wheels. It is pulled by a car
There were no houses. The families lived in caravans.

canoe a long, light boat, you use a paddle to move it
He paddled the canoe up the river.

card a piece of thick paper with pictures, sent for birthdays and Christmas
I like to get cards on my birthday.

care look after
Mother took care of me when I was ill.

cap a soft, flat hat
He did not wear his school cap.

carol a song sung at Christmas
I love to sing carols at Christmas.

carpet a thick cover put on the floor
My aunt has a carpet on the floor of her house.

31

A a B b **C c** D d E e F f G g H h I i J j K k L l M m

carrot a long, orange vegetable
Hares like to eat carrots.

carry lift something from one place to another
Please carry my bag. It is very heavy.

cart a wooden box on wheels that a man or an animal pulls
The donkey pulled the cart slowly up the hill.

carve cut wood or stone into a shape
The man carved a mask from a piece of wood.

case a box
John bought a case of beer for the party.

cat a small, furry animal with sharp claws, it is kept as a pet
My cat has a dish of milk every morning.

catch stop something that is moving and hold on to it
I'll throw the ball and you can catch it.

caterpillar a worm-like creature with many legs, it turns into a butterfly or a moth
The fat, ugly caterpillar turned into a beautiful butterfly.

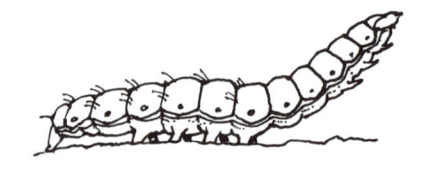

cattle cows or bulls, they give meat and milk
The rain has been heavy. The cattle will have plenty of food.

N n O o P p Q q R r S s T t U u V v W w X x Y y Z z

cave a big hole under the ground or in the side of a mountain
The lioness lives with her cubs in a cave.

cement a mixture of lime and sand, it holds bricks together
They built the wall with bricks and cement.

centre the middle part or point
That point is the centre of the circle.

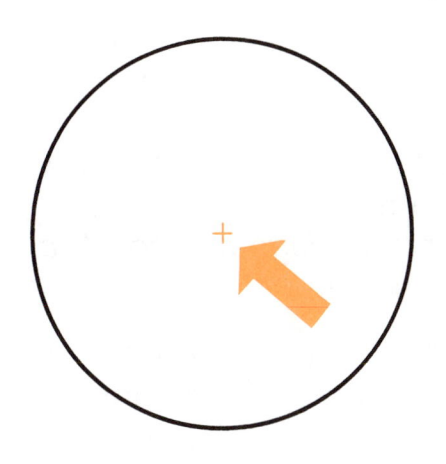

century one hundred years
We are now living in the twentieth century.

certain completely sure
I am certain that man stole my bicycle.

chain a row of metal rings joined together
The policeman put a chain around the prisoner's leg.

chair a seat with a back, for only one person
He sat down on a chair.

chalk 1 a soft white rock
The stones were made of chalk.
2 a soft white stick used for writing on the chalkboard
The teacher used the chalk to draw a map on the board.

change 1 money given back to you when you have paid too much
Mary put the change in her purse.
2 make or become different
The caterpillar changed into a butterfly.

chase run after someone or something
The cat chased the mouse around the room.

cheap at a low price
The eggs were cheap because some were broken.

33

A a B b **C c** D d E e F f G g H h I i J j K k L l M m

cheek the side of the face below the eye
John's cheek was sore. He had a bad tooth.

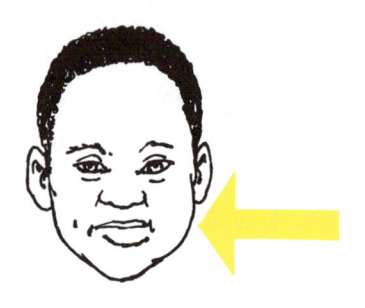

cheer a loud, happy shout
The crowd cheered when their team won.

cheese a food made from milk
Goats' cheese has a very strong taste.

cheetah a large, wild, spotted cat
The cheetah is the fastest animal in the world.

chest 1 a big, strong box
The old man kept his money in a chest.

2 the front part of the body between the neck and the waist
The boxer had a broad chest.

chew break food with your teeth
Chicken legs are good to chew on.

chicken a young hen. We eat its meat and eggs
The chickens have laid a lot of eggs this week.

N n O o P p Q q R r S s T t U u V v W w X x Y y Z z

child a young boy or girl
She is only a child. Don't beat her.

chimney a tall pipe inside the house, it takes away the smoke from the fire
The smoke from the chimney made everyone cough.

chimpanzee an animal like a monkey with no tail
Chimpanzees are easy to train.

chin the part of the face below the mouth
My brother's chin is covered with hair.

chip 1 a small piece of potato that is fried in oil
I like ketchup on my chips.
2 a small piece that has been broken off
My sister chipped the cup when she hit it with a knife.

chocolate a sweet brown food made from cocoa and sugar
Mother gave me a piece of chocolate for my lunch.

choose take one thing from a number of things
Which pencil will you choose? The red one or the blue one?

chop cut with an axe
The man chopped the tree down.

Christ one of Jesus' other names
Christmas is Jesus Christ's birthday.

church a building where people go to sing and pray to God
I go to church every Sunday.

cinema a building where people go to see films
Father is taking us to the cinema tonight.

35

A a B b **C c** D d E e F f G g H h I i J j K k L l M m

circle a round shape
Rings and wheels are all made in the shape of a circle.

city a very large town
My uncle lives in Gaborone. It is a city.

clap make a noise by hitting your hands together
We all clapped when father got his prize.

class a group of people who learn things together
The teacher told the class to write a story about a lion.

claw a hard, sharp nail that some birds and animals have on their feet
The cat held the mouse in its claws.

clay a sticky soil used for making bricks
The man left the clay bricks in the sun to dry.

clean 1 not dirty
The water in the river was clean.
2 make something clean
Jane helped to clean the windows.

clever able to learn and understand things quickly
Alan is very clever. He is always first in our class.

cliff the steep side of a mountain or hill
The boy fell down the cliff and broke his leg.

climb go up a steep place using your hands and feet
The boy climbed the tree to get the apples.

N n O o P p Q q R r S s T t U u V v W w X x Y y Z z

clock a machine that shows the time
I have a clock beside my bed.

close 1 shut
Please close the door.
2 very near
My uncle lives close to us.

cloth a piece of material for cleaning
Mother used a cloth to wipe the table.

clothes the things you wear to cover your body
My sister has lots of pretty clothes.

cloud the black or white shapes made from drops of water that float in the sky
Look at the black clouds. It is going to rain.

clown someone who wears funny clothes and makes people laugh
The clown wore a big bright nose.

coast the place where the land meets the sea
The coast of Kenya is beautiful.

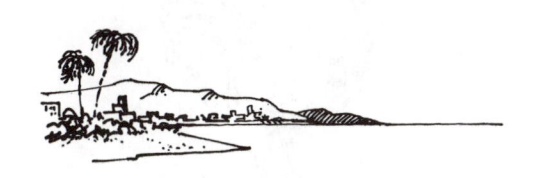

coat something that you wear over your clothes to keep you warm and dry
It is very cold today. My mother is wearing her coat.

cobweb an old web made by a spider, it is covered in dust
There were lots of cobwebs in the corners of the room.

37

A a B b **C c** D d E e F f G g H h I i J j K k L l M m

---

cock a male bird
The cock chased the hens out of the yard.

cocoa a brown powder, it is made from a bean
Mother made us a drink of hot milk and cocoa.

coffee a hot drink made from the beans of a bush
Father has coffee every morning.

cold not hot
I will light the fire. It is very cold today.

collar a band round the neck of a shirt or coat
I have a blue shirt with a white collar.

colour 1 red, blue and yellow are colours
What is the colour of your new hat?
      2 put paint or crayon on something
I am going to colour the box red.

colt a young male horse
Father has taken the colt to the field.

comb a piece of plastic or wood with a row of thin teeth, we use it to tidy our hair
Mother told her to go and comb her hair.

come 1 move towards a person or thing
Come over here and look at this bird.
      2 arrive
Has the bus come yet?

compass a machine with a needle that always points north
We used the compass to find our way.

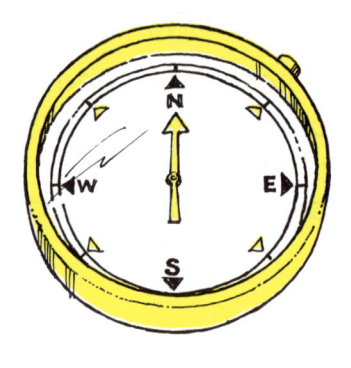

concrete a mixture of cement and stones used for building
The new bridge is made of concrete.

N n O o P p Q q R r S s T t U u V v W w X x Y y Z z

container a box, bottle, can or jar used for holding things
The farmer put the container of milk on the back of the lorry.

cook make food ready to eat by heating it
Mother is cooking fish for dinner.

cool not warm, nearly cold
The water is too hot. Wait until it is cool.

copy make one thing the same as another
She copied the letter into her book.

corn seeds of a plant grown for food
The corn is ready to go to the mill.

corner a place where two walls or streets meet
He drove the car too fast around the corner and had an accident.

correct 1 with no mistakes
All my answers were correct.
2 make right
The teacher corrected the test.

cot a baby's bed with high sides and bars
The baby was crying in its cot.

count say numbers in order
The boys can both count very well.

country 1 a land with its own people and laws
Botswana, Zambia and Kenya are all countries.
2 open areas of land outside towns
At weekends we drive into the country.

A a B b **C c** D d E e F f G g H h I i J j K k L l M m

cover put a blanket or paper over
She covered the little boy with the blanket.

cow a large female animal kept for its milk and beef
He gets up early in the morning to milk the cows.

crab a water animal with big claws and a hard shell
Crab meat is good to eat.

crane 1 a machine with a big arm which lifts heavy objects
The crane lifted the heavy pipe on to the lorry.

2 a bird with long legs and a long beak that eats fish
The crane caught the fish in its beak.

N n O o P p Q q R r S s T t U u V v W w X x Y y Z z

crawl 1 move very slowly
The bus crawled up the steep hill.
    2 move on your hands and knees
The baby crawled across the floor.

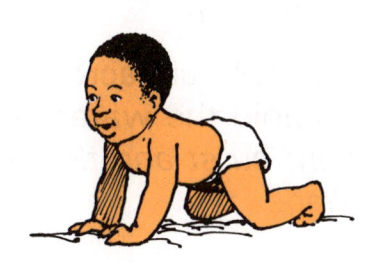

crayon a small stick of coloured wax used for drawing
I am going to draw a ship with my crayons.

cream the thick, yellow part of the milk
Butter is made from cream.

cricket an insect like a grasshopper
Crickets make a noise by rubbing their wings together.

crisp 1 very thin slices of fried potato
I would like a bag of potato crisps.
    2 very dry and easy to break
These biscuits are very crisp.

crocodile a large reptile with sharp teeth, they live beside rivers
A crocodile has a thick skin, short legs and a long tail.

crooked not straight, bent
We could not use the piece of wood. It was crooked.

cross 1 a shape or mark like this + or this x
You can see a cross in the church.
    2 angry
Father was cross when the car would not start.

crow a big black bird
The crow chased away the small birds.

crowd a lot of people all together
There was a large crowd at the football match.

crown a ring of gold or silver worn on the head of a queen or king
The king appeared wearing his gold crown.

cruel enjoy hurting a person or animal
The cruel man was kicking the dog.

41

A a B b **C c** D d E e F f G g H h I i J j K k L l M m

crust the hard skin on the outside of something
I like the crust of the bread.

cry 1 shout or call loudly
'There is a snake in the garden,' cried the boy.
   2 when tears fall from your eyes
I always cry when I cut onions.

cup a small round bowl with a handle
Mother made us all a cup of coffee.

cupboard a large box to put things in. It has a door and shelves
Mother opened the cupboard. It was full of tins, bottles and bags of flour.

curve a line that is not straight, it looks like the letter C or U
The road up the mountain had many curves in it.

cut 1 shape with an object like a knife
She cut the picture out of the newspaper.
   2 an opening made in the skin by a sharp object
He cut his finger on the knife.

Dd

dad another name for father
My dad works in an office.

dairy a place where milk is made into cheese and butter
The farmer takes his milk to the dairy. They make it into cheese for him.

dam a wall built across a river to hold the water back
The dam burst and flooded the village.

damage break something
The car was badly damaged in the crash.

damp a little wet
She wiped the dishes with a damp cloth.

N n O o P p Q q R r S s T t U u V v W w X x Y y Z z

dance move your body in time to music
I love to dance to quick music.

danger a thing that could kill or hurt you
It is dangerous to play on the road.

dare ask someone to show they are brave
I dare you to ride that wild horse.

dark without much light, nearly black
It was very dark that night.

date 1 a day, month and year
What is the date of your birthday?
2 the small, brown, sweet fruit of the palm tree
I was eating dates. My hands were sticky.

daughter a female child
My aunt has three daughters.

day 1 the twenty-four hours from one midnight to the next
The baby was kept in hospital for three days.
2 the part of the day between sunrise and sunset
The sun shone all day.

dead no longer alive
The dead cat lay at the side of the road.

deaf not able to hear
The old man was deaf. He did not hear the car coming.

dear 1 loved
I have a dear little puppy.
2 costing a lot of money
That radio is too dear. I cannot buy it.

December the last month of the year
We have school holidays in December.

decide choose to do something
I cannot decide which dress to wear.

43

A a B b C c **D d** E e F f G g H h I i J j K k L l M m

decimal using tens in arithmetic
Write it down as a decimal not a fraction.

deep going down a long way
The miners worked deep underground digging out the coal.

deer a very quick animal with beautiful horns
The hyena could not catch the deer.

den a cave or home for wild animals
The jackal hid in its den.

dentist someone who looks after people's teeth
The dentist will take good care of your teeth.

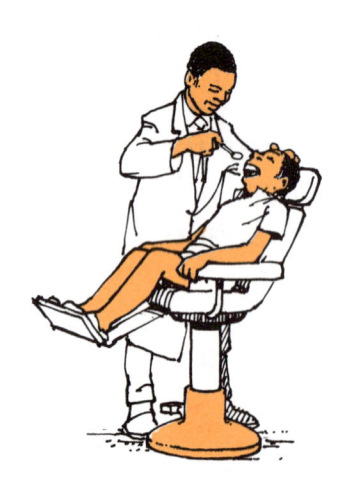

describe say what someone or something is like
Can you describe the man who stole your bag?

desert a large dry place where few plants can grow
Camels are the only animals which can cross the desert.

desk a table for writing or reading
The boy did his homework at his desk.

destroy make something useless by breaking or damaging it
The fire destroyed the house.

devil a very bad person
In the Bible the devil is called Satan.

dew tiny drops of water which form on things during the night
The dog left its footprints in the dew.

44

N n O o P p Q q R r S s T t U u V v W w X x Y y Z z

diagonal a line drawn from one corner of something to the opposite corner
The flag had two narrow diagonal lines.

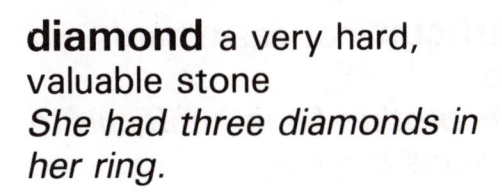

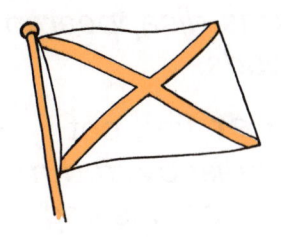

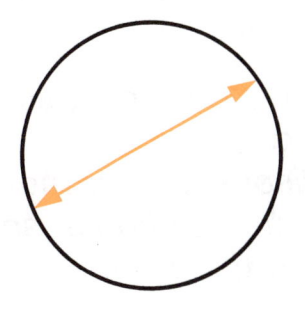

diamond a very hard, valuable stone
She had three diamonds in her ring.

dial a circle with numbers around it
Clocks, watches and telephones all have dials.

diameter a straight line from one side of a circle to the other, it goes through the middle
The wheel was fifty centimetres in diameter.

diary a book in which you write down the things which happen to you every day
Jane has kept a diary for the last five years.

dice a small six-sided block of wood or plastic, it has dots from one to six on each side
Dice are used in many board games.

dictionary a book in which you can find out how to spell a word and what it means
Using a dictionary helps you to learn English.

die stop living
The maize will die if it does not rain.

different not the same as
A square is different from a circle.

A a B b C c **D d** E e F f G g H h I i J j K k L l M m

difficult not easy, hard to do
My brother finds it difficult to ride his bicycle.

dig make a hole in the ground
Before planting the tree the men must dig a hole.

dim almost dark, very little light
There was a dim light coming from the window.

dinner the main meal of the day
Come to my house for dinner tonight.

dinosaur a large animal which lived on the earth millions of years ago
There are no dinosaurs alive today.

direction the way you go to get to a place
Which direction is north?

dirty covered with mud or stains
Take off that dirty dress.

disappear go away and not be seen
The birds disappeared into the clouds.

discover find out
When I discovered my bicycle was missing I went to the police.

dish a shallow bowl for food
Mother put the dish of stew on the table.

dishonest not telling the truth, not honest
It is dishonest to tell lies.

dislike not like, hate someone or something
I dislike eating porridge in the morning.

disobey not doing as you are told
She disobeyed her mother. She didn't go home, she went to the cinema.

N n O o P p Q q R r S s T t U u V v W w X x Y y Z z

distance the space between two places
What is the distance from Gaborone to Lusaka?

disturb upset someone, waken them up
Do not disturb me. I am going to sleep.

ditch a long, narrow hole in the ground, it takes rainwater away
Ditches prevent flooding.

dive jump head first into the water
My brother hurt his head when he dived into the pool.

divide 1 find out how many times one number goes into another
If you divide six by two you get three.
2 break into smaller parts
Please divide the cake into four parts.

dizzy a strange feeling, as if everything is turning around
I felt dizzy as I looked down from the top of the tall tree.

do start and finish a job
I will do my homework early tomorrow.

dock a place where ships stay in the harbour
The passenger ship tied up at the dock.

doctor a man or woman who makes sick people well
The doctor gave me medicine for my headache.

dog a four-legged animal which is often kept as a pet
The dog barked at the boy on the bicycle.

doll a toy, it looks like a person
Her mother made a new dress for her doll.

domino a piece of wood with dots on it. It is used in a game
Would you like to play dominoes?

donkey an animal like a small horse with big ears
Donkeys are small but they carry large loads.

A a B b C c **D d** E e F f G g H h I i J j K k L l M m

door a flat piece of wood, it fills an opening in a wall – you can open or close a door
He closed the door to keep the room warm.

dose an amount of medicine
Take a dose of the medicine when you get home.

dot a small round mark
Remember to put a dot over your i's.

double twice as many or twice as much
The price of butter is double what it was last year.

doubt when you are not sure of something
I doubt that I can jump the wall.

dove a bird that looks like a pigeon
The doves flew up into the tree.

down from a higher place to a lower place
He ran down the hill.

doze be almost asleep
Father likes to doze after dinner.

dozen twelve of anything
Mother bought a dozen eggs in the shop.

drag pull something along the ground
He dragged the sack of potatoes to the barn.

drain a pipe to take away water
He poured the dirty water down the drain.

drake a male duck
My sister likes to feed the ducks and drakes with bread.

draw 1 make a picture with a crayon or pencil
The boy is going to draw a picture of an elephant.
2 end a game with both sides having the same score
The two teams drew 2-2 on Wednesday.

N n O o P p Q q R r S s T t U u V v W w X x Y y Z z

drawer a box with no lid which slides into and out of a piece of furniture
Mother put father's clean shirts in the drawer.

dream things that you hear and see when you are sleeping
Some dreams are happy and some are sad.

dress 1 put your clothes on
Jane dressed her doll.
2 a piece of clothing, it is like a shirt and skirt joined together
My teacher was wearing a brown dress today.

dribble 1 when a little liquid runs out of your mouth
Babies always dribble.
2 keeping a ball close to your feet as you run
The young players are learning how to dribble the ball.

drill a tool with a sharp metal point for making holes
Father drilled holes in the wood.

drink swallow liquid
Please don't drink all the water.

drip fall slowly in small drops
The rain dripped from the trees.

drive make an animal or machine move
I will drive you to the station in my uncle's car.

49

A a B b C c **D d** E e F f G g H h I i J j K k L l M m

drizzle very fine rain
It drizzled all weekend.

drop 1 a small spot of liquid
Only a few drops of rain came from the black cloud.
    2 let something fall
The man dropped the brick on his foot.

drown die underwater without air
Many people drowned when the ship sank.

drum a round, hollow box, you hit it with your hands or a stick to make music
David plays the drum in the band.

dry not wet
Always light a fire with dry wood.

duck a bird which likes to swim in water
The duck took her babies into the water.

dumb not able to talk
There are special schools for dumb people.

during at the same time as something else is going on
She fell asleep during the film.

dust the tiny pieces of dirt which float in the air
Mother used a cloth to wipe the dust off the table.

dwarf a very short person
The dwarf sat in the child's chair.

dye change the colour of something
We will dye these white sheets blue.

Ee

each every person or thing
Each child has a pencil.

eagle a large bird with a hooked beak and sharp claws, it eats small animals
The eagle caught the snake in its claws.

ear the part of the head used for hearing
An elephant has very large ears.

50

N n O o P p Q q R r S s T t U u V v W w X x Y y Z z

early 1 near the beginning of
The athlete fell early in the race.
      2 before the usual time
The rains came early this year.

earn get money for the work that you do
He earns money every week by watering the garden.

earth 1 the planet that we live on
How many people live on the Earth?
      2 soil
Crops need good earth to grow in.

earthquake a sudden shaking of the earth's crust
The city was destroyed by the earthquake.

easel a stand for holding a chalkboard or a picture
They put the picture on an easel.

east where the sun rises in the morning
The sun rises in the east and sets in the west.

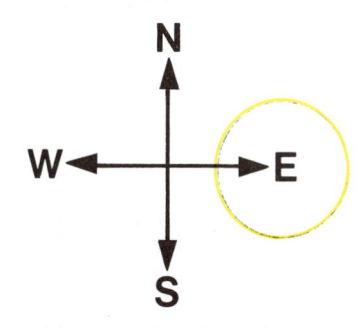

Easter the time when Christ died and then lived again
Easter Sunday is a joyful day for Christians.

easy not difficult, not hard to do
Our homework was easy tonight.

eat chew food and swallow it
Mother told us to eat all our potatoes.

51

A a B b C c D d **E e** F f G g H h I i J j K k L l M m

echo the sound of your voice that comes back to you from a hill or in a cave
My voice echoed around the cave.

edge the place where a thing ends
The boy played at the edge of the river.

educate teach or train someone
We go to school to be educated.

egg an oval object with a shell, some baby animals and birds are born in them
We eat hens' eggs.

eight the number 8
Eight people got off the bus.

eighteen the number 18
My uncle bought eighteen goats yesterday.

eighty the number 80
Some elephants are eighty years old.

either when there are two things, you must choose one
We will take either the taxi or the bus.

elastic a strip of rubber material. You can stretch it
His trousers were held up by an elastic belt.

elbow the part in the middle of the arm where it bends
When he bent his arm his elbow was sore.

elder older
He is my elder brother.

electricity power that moves along wires giving light and heat. It makes machines work
Power lines carry electricity across the country.

elephant a very large animal with big ears, tusks and a long nose called a trunk
Elephants use their trunks to pull leaves off trees.

N n O o P p Q q R r S s T t U u V v W w X x Y y Z z

empty with nothing inside
The family moved into the empty house.

encyclopedia a book or a lot of books which tell you about all sorts of things
They have got encyclopedias in the school library.

end finish
The teacher came to the end of the story.

enemy a person or country that wants to hurt or fight you
The two countries have been enemies for years.

engine a machine that uses its own power to move things
It took two engines to pull the heavy train.

enjoy be happy doing something
I enjoy singing in the church.

enough as much or as many as are needed
Have we got enough food for everyone?

entrance the way into a place
The entrance to the house had iron gates.

envelope a paper cover for a letter
She wrote the address on the envelope.

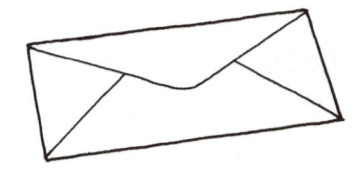

escape get free or get away
The prisoners escaped from the policemen.

evening the part of the day between the afternoon and the night
Birds fly back to their nests in the evening.

53

A a B b C c D d **E e** F f G g H h I i J j K k L l M m

ever at any time
Have you ever caught a fish?

every each or all
The shop is open every day.

examination 1 an important test of your work
Sally got full marks in her English examination.
2 a close look at something or someone
The dentist made a careful examination of my sister's teeth.

excuse a reason for doing or not doing something
His excuse for being late was that his watch had stopped.

exercise 1 work that you do to help you learn
The teacher gave the class an exercise to do.
2 training that makes the body fit and healthy
They had an exercise class for all the mothers.

explain make something clear
The farmer explained how to milk the cow.

explode burst with a loud bang
The petrol tank caught fire and exploded.

explore have a careful look around a place for the first time
The boys had great fun exploring the caves.

eye the part of the head used for seeing
She had beautiful brown eyes.

Ff

face 1 the front part of the head
The dog had a furry face.
2 have the front towards something
Our house faces the school.

fact something that is true
This is a fact: the Earth goes round the Sun.

factory a place where people use machines to make things
My uncle works in a factory that makes cars.

N n O o P p Q q R r S s T t U u V v W w X x Y y Z z

fade become harder to see or hear
The sound of the cars faded into the distance.

fail try to do something but be unable to do it
He failed to pass his history exam.

fair 1 light in colour
I have fair hair. My brother has black hair.
    2 good for everyone
Let's be fair. We will each have a piece of the cake.

fall drop down suddenly
He fell off the horse and hurt his leg.

family grandparents, parents and their children
My mother and father and brothers are my family.

famous very well-known
Everyone wanted to see the famous singer.

far a long way off
Africa is far from America.

fare the money you pay to travel on a bus, train, taxi, boat or plane
Mary paid the bus fare into town.

farm a piece of land where a farmer grows crops and keeps animals
The farmer keeps cattle and goats on his farm.

fast quick or quickly
He drives his car too fast.

fasten close something so that it will not open
Please fasten the gate to keep the cows in.

fat 1 a person who is very round
My aunt eats too much. She is very fat.

    2 the white part of meat
Please cut the fat off the meat before cooking it.

55

A a B b C c D d E e **F f** G g H h I i J j K k L l M m

---

father a male parent
My father is a teacher.

fault something wrong with a person or thing
There is a fault in the cooker. It is not working.

favourite something or someone you like best
Red is my favourite colour.

feather one of the small light things that cover a bird's body
Some of the hens had brown feathers.

fear feeling afraid
The children saw the lion. They began to shake with fear.

February the second month of the year
My sister's birthday is in February.

feeble very weak
The old lady felt very feeble after her illness.

feed give a person or animal food
I will feed the dog tonight.

female any person or animal that can have babies
Sows are female pigs.

fence a wall made of wood or wire
We have a wooden fence around our field.

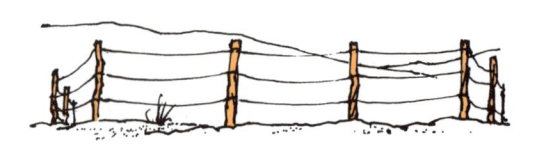

ferry a boat. It takes people, lorries and cars across water
The ferry carried the lorries across the river.

few not very many
There were only a few seats left on the bus. Most of us had to stand.

field a piece of land with a fence around it. You can grow crops or grass there
We have a good field of corn this year.

fierce angry and cruel
Do not go into the shed. There is a fierce dog in there.

fifteen the number 15
Joe is fifteen years old today.

fifty the number 50
It is fifty kilometres to the next town.

N n O o P p Q q R r S s T t U u V v W w X x Y y Z z

fight take part in a row
My brother always fights over the biggest piece of cake.

figure 1 a number
1, 2 and 3 are all figures.
2 the shape of a body
The figure of the man disappeared into the night.

fill make something full
They filled the tank of the car with petrol.

fin a part of the body of a fish. Fins help the fish to swim
The fish used its fins to turn in the water.

find see something you were looking for
Can you find my coat?

finger one of the five long parts on the end of your hand
She wore a gold ring on her finger.

finish come to the end of something
You can go home when you have finished your work.

fire the heat and flames that come from burning things
Joe lit the fire to cook the meat.

firm 1 a group of people who have a business
He works for a firm of builders.
2 fixed so that it will not move
We fixed the shelf firmly to the wall.

first before anyone else, in front of everyone else
She sat in the first row so that she could see better.

fish 1 an animal with scales and fins that lives and breathes underwater
The lake was full of fish.
2 try and catch fish
Father is going to fish in the lake.

57

A a B b C c D d E e **F f** G g H h I i J j K k L l M m

fist the hand when all the fingers are closed
The two boys were having a fist fight.

fit be the right shape or size
The dress did not fit me, it was too small.

five the number 5
She bought five apples.

fix 1 mend
My father fixed the puncture on his bicycle.
2 join firmly
The picture was fixed firmly to the wall.

flag a piece of coloured cloth fixed to a pole
Every country has its flag.

flame the white and yellow burning part of a fire
The flames were jumping from the fire.

flamingo a bird with long legs, a long neck and pink and red feathers
The flamingos rose like a pink cloud into the sky.

flap move up and down like the wings of a bird
The washing was flapping in the wind.

flash a sudden bright light
A flash of light could be seen in the dark sky.

flat 1 smooth and level
The men tried to make the road flat.
2 a home, some rooms inside a big house or building
My uncle and aunt live in a block of flats.

flight flying in the air
When the guns went off the birds took flight.

float stay up in the air, stay on the top of water without sinking
The balloon floated up into the clouds.

flock a large group of birds or sheep
The flock of sheep has eaten all the grass.

flood too much water in a river or on the land
The river has flooded the fields.

N n O o P p Q q R r S s T t U u V v W w X x Y y Z z

floor the part of the room you walk on
The lady next door has a new carpet on her floor.

flour a powder made from grain used to make cakes and bread
Mother bought 5 kg of brown flour to make bread.

flow move smoothly like a river
The river flows into the sea.

flower the coloured part of the plant. It turns into the seed and the fruit
The flowers on the apple tree are pretty.

fly 1 a small insect with one pair of wings
He closed the window to keep the flies out.

2 move through the air
I am going to fly to London next week.

fog a thick mist
You could not see the trees because of the fog.

fold bend or turn something so that one part is on top of the other
I folded the letter to put it in the envelope.

follow come or go after someone or something
The cows followed the old man home.

food the things that people and animals eat
I hope we have enough food for the party.

fool someone who does silly things
Only a fool would climb that high cliff.

foot the part of your body that you stand on
She cut her foot on the broken bottle.

A a B b C c D d E e **F f** G g H h I i J j K k L l M m

football a team game. You kick a ball and get goals
My brother's in the school football team.

forehead the part of your face over your eyes
He brushed his hair back from his forehead.

forest a big piece of land with many trees on it
Many trees in the forest were cut down for firewood.

forget fail to remember
I forgot to brush my teeth.

forgive stop being angry with someone
Please forgive me for breaking the vase.

form a printed paper with spaces to write on
We had to fill in the doctor's form.

fortnight two weeks
We are going on holiday for a fortnight.

forty the number 40
There were forty children in our class.

forward to the front
The car moved slowly forward.

fountain a jet of water that shoots up into the air
There was a fountain in front of the house.

four the number 4.
A chair has four legs.

fourteen the number 14
There are fourteen days in a fortnight.

fowl a bird, we eat its eggs and meat
Hens and cocks are fowls.

fracture break
He fell and fractured his arm.

frame put a firm edge around something
That picture needs a new frame.

60

N n O o P p Q q R r S s T t U u V v W w X x Y y Z z

free 1 able to move and act without being stopped by anyone or anything
Birds should not be kept in cages. They should be free.
2 costing nothing
If you buy six litres of petrol you get free oil.

fresh something made, grown or caught a short time ago
We are having fresh fish for dinner.

Friday the sixth day of the week
I go to school from Monday to Friday.

friend a person you like and know well
He is my best friend.

fright sudden fear
The snake gave the little girl a fright.

frog a small animal that jumps and lives on land and in water
Baby frogs are called tadpoles.

from where something started
He flew from Kenya to London.

front the part of the person or thing we see first
I spilt my tea down the front of my shirt.

frontier the line between two countries
The river was the frontier between the two countries.

frown have lines on your forehead when you are angry or thinking very hard
The teacher frowned at the naughty boy.

fruit the seed of the plant, the soft part around the seed
Apples, bananas and oranges are types of fruits.

fry cook in hot oil or fat
Chips are fried slices of potato.

full hold as much or as many as possible
The jug was full of milk.

fun enjoy doing something
We had great fun at the party.

61

A a B b C c D d E e **F f** G g H h I i J j K k L l M m

fur the soft, thick hair that covers some animals
Leopards have spotted fur.

furniture beds, tables and chairs that you use inside the house
Mother bought some new furniture for the house.

Gg

gain have something you did not have before
He has gained good results in his school work.

gale a very strong wind
The trees blew down in the gale.

gallop like a horse going very fast
The horse galloped across the field.

game a sport or something that you play that has rules
Football and dominoes are games.

gang a group of people who do things together
The gang of workmen mended the road.

gap a space or opening
The horse escaped through the gap in the fence.

garage 1 a building in which you keep your car
I put my car in the garage.

2 a place which sells petrol and mends cars
Please take the car to the garage. It needs some petrol.

garden a piece of ground where people grow flowers, fruit and vegetables
I picked a basket of beans from the garden.

gas something like air
We cook our food on a gas cooker.

N n O o P p Q q R r S s T t U u V v W w X x Y y Z z

gasp breathe quickly because you are tired
The boy gasped for breath after swimming under water.

gate a door in a wall or fence
Shut the gate or the dog will get out.

gather come together
The people gathered in the church.

gear 1 a part of a car or bicycle, it makes the wheels turn
He put the car in a low gear to get it up the hill.
2 the things you need for a job or a sport
He left his fishing gear on the bus.

gentle quiet and kind
The cat lifted the kitten gently in its mouth.

geography learning about the countries of the world
We were learning about Australia in our Geography class today.

get take or buy something
Can you get me the newspaper from the table?

giant a very large man in a fairy story
The giant was as tall as a tree.

giraffe an African animal with a very long neck
The giraffe bent its long neck to eat the leaves off the small bush.

girl a young female
The girls' netball team won their match.

give let someone have something
Mother gave me money to buy some milk.

glacier a slow-moving river of ice
The glacier moved slowly down the mountain.

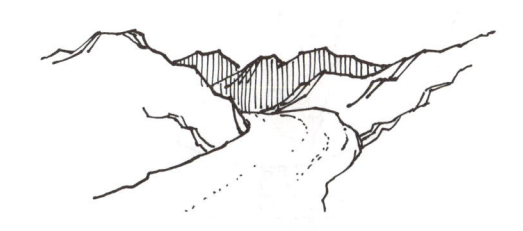

63

A a B b C c D d E e F f **G g** H h I i J j K k L l M m

glad pleased or happy
After the long journey we were glad to arrive home.

glass a hard material, you can see through it
We use glass to make windows.

glasses pieces of glass to help you see better
My sister wears glasses for reading.

glide move smoothly
The boat glided across the water.

globe a ball with a map of the world on it
Can you find Lusaka on the globe?

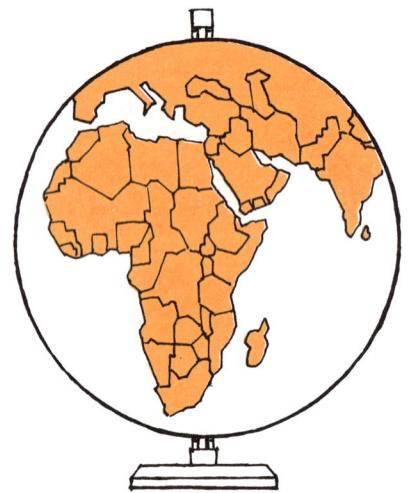

glove the clothes you wear on your hands
She wore gloves in the cold weather.

go move or travel
We will go and buy the vegetables for the stew.

goal 1 the two posts that the ball must go between to score in football
Mike kicked the ball into the goal.
2 a point won in football and other games
The red team won by two goals.

goat a four-legged animal with horns. We eat its milk and meat
Goats often have a strong smell.

64

N n O o P p Q q R r S s T t U u V v W w X x Y y Z z

god someone or something that people worship
Long ago people believed the sun was a god.

gold a shining yellow metal that is very valuable
Gold can be found in rivers and under the ground.

good 1 kind, nice
He is a good boy.
2 do things very well
He is a very good swimmer.

goodbye a word you use when you are leaving someone
She said goodbye to her mother.

goods things that you can buy or sell
The goods were sent to the shop on a lorry.

gorilla the largest and strongest of the ape-like animals
Gorillas are very gentle as long as you do not make them angry.

graceful moving beautifully
The lady danced gracefully around the room.

grandfather the father of your father or mother
My grandfather died long ago.

grandmother the mother of your mother or father
My grandmother is seventy years old.

grape a small green or purple fruit. It grows in bunches
We can eat grapes or make them into wine.

grass a low green plant. Many animals eat it
The cows ate the grass in the field.

A a B b C c D d E e F f **G** g H h I i J j K k L l M m

grasshopper a green, jumping insect with long legs
The grasshopper jumped into the house.

grateful feeling or showing thanks to a person
The man was very grateful for the food.

gravy a brown sauce, we make it from the juice of cooked meat
I like gravy on my potatoes.

grease a thick oil or fat
We rubbed grease on his bicycle chain.

great big, important or famous
That man is a great footballer.

greedy want more of something than you need
Do not take any more sweets. You are just greedy.

green the colour of new grass or leaves
Apples can be green or red.

grey the colour you get when you mix black and white
Elephants are grey.

grin a wide smile
You could tell the boy was happy because he had a broad grin.

grocer someone who sells different types of food and other goods for the house
Mother sent me to the grocer to buy some tea and matches.

ground the surface of the earth
The large tree fell to the ground.

group a number of people or things, they belong together
The teacher took a group of schoolchildren to the cinema.

grow 1 become bigger
Sam has grown into a big boy.
        2 plant seeds or flowers in your garden
We will grow cabbages in the garden this year.

grown-up adult, a man or woman
She has a grown-up son.

guard keep a person or place safe
We have two dogs to guard our house.

N n O o P p Q q R r S s T t U u V v W w X x Y y Z z

guess try to answer when you are not sure
Can you guess what is in this box?

guide a person who shows people the way to go
The guide showed them the way over the mountain.

guilty when you have done something wrong
The man was guilty of stealing the money.

gum 1 the part of your mouth where the teeth grow
Your gums bleed when you lose a tooth.
2 a sweet to chew. You do not swallow it
I like to chew gum. It helps me to think.

gun a weapon with a hollow metal tube for firing bullets
The man fired the gun in the air to make the birds go away.

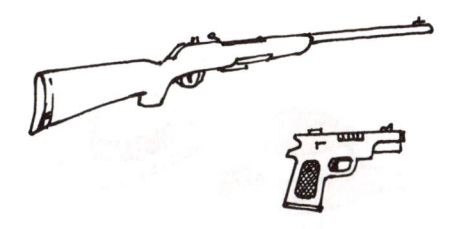

Hh

hair a soft covering, it grows on the heads and bodies of people and animals
His mother said, 'Get your hair cut!'

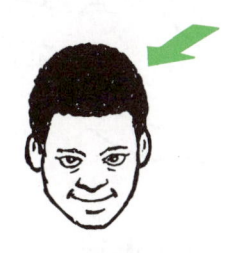

half one of two parts that are exactly the same
He took half of the orange and gave his sister half.

hall a large room or building for meetings
The meeting was held in the town hall.

hammer a tool for hitting nails
He hammered the nails into the wood.

67

A a B b C c D d E e F f G g **H h** I i J j K k L l M m

hand the part of the body at the end of the arm
The children clapped their hands in time to the music.

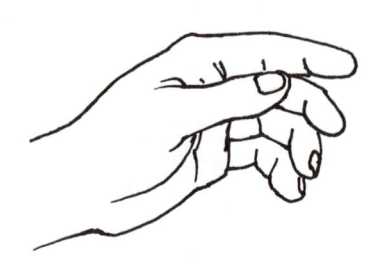

handkerchief a piece of cloth for cleaning your nose
Brian blew his nose on a red handkerchief.

handle the part of a thing you hold with your hand
The handle of the spade is broken.

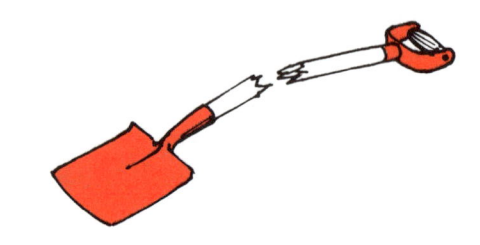

handsome good-looking
She had a handsome son with brown eyes and curly hair.

hang to fix the top part of something to a hook or nail
I will hang the washing on the line.

happen take place
The accident happened when it was raining.

happy joyful, pleased
The children were very happy to have a holiday.

harbour a safe place for ships to tie up
There were ten big ships in the harbour.

hard 1 firm like metal
He hurt himself on the hard rock.
   2 difficult, not easy
Our homework is very hard.

hare an animal like a large rabbit
Some people keep hares and rabbits for food.

harvest the crops a farmer gathers
Father will have a good maize harvest this year.

hat something you wear on your head
The girl's hat blew off in the wind.

N n O o P p Q q R r S s T t U u V v W w X x Y y Z z

hate dislike someone or something very much
I hate to clean my shoes every day.

have belong to, own
I have four goats and two cows.

hawk a bird that hunts small animals
The hawk flew down and caught the rabbit in its claws.

hay the dry grass used to feed animals
After the harvest the barn will be full of hay.

head the part of the body with the eyes, nose, ears and mouth
He had a big hat on his head.

health how ill or well you are
Don't smoke cigarettes and you will have good health.

heap a pile of things
Look at that heap of rubbish in the road.

hear use your ears
The radio is not very loud. I cannot hear it.

heart a part of the body, it pumps blood
He is an old man, but he has a strong heart.

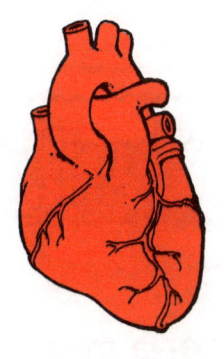

heat 1 the hot feeling from a fire or the sun
The heat from the sun dried the clothes.
2 make something hot
Heat the water for a cup of tea, please.

heaven the place where Christians believe God lives
Christians hope to see God in heaven.

69

A a B b C c D d E e F f G g **H h** I i J j K k L l M m

heavy weigh a lot, hard to lift
It is hard to lift heavy things.

hedge a wall of bushes
Father is growing a hedge round his house.

helicopter a machine for flying. It can fly straight up and down
The police followed the thieves in a helicopter.

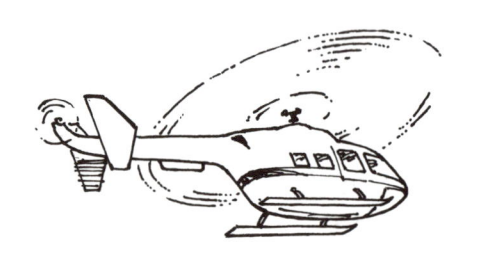

hello a word you say when you meet someone
'Hello,' he said. 'Are you going to school?'

helmet a hard hat to keep your head safe
Miners always wear helmets.

help do something for someone
Help your mother to carry that box.

hem the edge of a dress, it is sewn
Mother sewed the hem of my new dress.

hen a female bird, we eat some hens and their eggs
All the hens laid eggs today.

herd a group of animals
The herd of cattle drank at the water hole.

here this place
Come here. I want to talk to you.

hero a very brave man
The hero rescued the baby from the river.

N n O o P p Q q R r S s T t U u V v W w X x Y y Z z

heron a water bird with long legs
The heron caught a frog in its beak.

hide find a secret place
We can hide in the old cave.

high a long way up
The eagle flew high into the sky.

hill a high piece of ground
You can see our village from the top of the hill.

hippopotamus a large African animal that lives in water
The hippopotamus lives in the river. The water keeps it cool.

hiss make a sound like a snake
The snake hissed. It was very angry.

hit give someone a hard smack
The boy hit the ball into the river.

hive a bee's home
All the bees have left their hive.

hoe a garden tool. It digs out weeds
The gardener used the hoe to dig out the weeds.

hold have in your hands
Please hold the baby for me.

71

A a B b C c D d E e F f G g **H h** I i J j K k L l M m

hole an opening in the ground
The men dug a hole in the street.

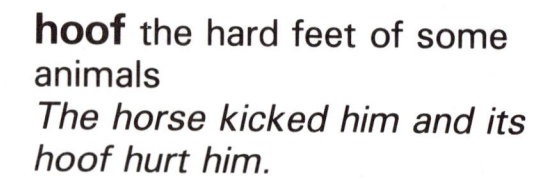

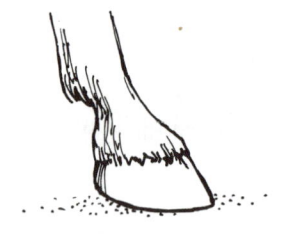

hoof the hard feet of some animals
The horse kicked him and its hoof hurt him.

hook a piece of bent metal for hanging things on or catching things
He bent the nail to make a hook.

holiday days off from school
We have a holiday on Saturday and Sunday.

home the place where you live
I want to go home to see my mother.

honest telling the truth, not stealing
An honest person never tells lies.

honey the sweet food made by bees
I like honey on my bread.

hoop a big metal or wooden ring
The dog jumped through the burning hoop.

N n O o P p Q q R r S s T t U u V v W w X x Y y Z z

hop jump on one foot
The girl hopped across the room.

hope want something to happen
I hope to get a bicycle for Christmas.

horn a pointed bone. It grows on the heads of some animals
Cows, goats and buffaloes have horns.

horse a four-legged animal, we ride them and they pull carts
The man rode his horse to bring in the sheep.

hose a long tube of rubber or plastic, water goes through it
We need the hose to water the vegetables.

hospital a place where doctors and nurses help sick people
Jack is in hospital with a broken leg.

hot very warm
Is the soup hot enough to eat?

hotel a building, you can pay to sleep and eat there
We stayed in a very nice hotel for two days.

hour sixty minutes
The cake will take an hour to bake.

house a building, people live in it
I would like to live in that house.

73

A a B b C c D d E e F f G g **H h** I i J j K k L l M m

how in what way?
How did you fix that broken chair?

howl the long, loud, crying sound of an animal
The howl of the hyenas was very frightening.

hug hold someone tightly in your arms
Mother saw her aunt. She ran and hugged her.

huge very big
They built a huge wall at the dam.

hum sing with your lips closed
The boy started to hum the song. He did not know the words.

human any man, woman or child
How many human beings are there on the earth?

hump a round lump
Camels have humps on their backs.

hundred the number 100
It is one hundred kilometres to the nearest town.

hungry feeling you need food
We eat when we are hungry.

hurry move quickly
Hurry or we will miss the bus.

hurt make a person or animal feel pain
I hurt my knee when I fell.

hut a small house
The farmer kept hens in the hut.

N n O o P p Q q R r S s T t U u V v W w X x Y y Z z

hyena a wild, dog-like animal, it eats meat and makes a laughing noise
The hyenas ate the dead zebra.

hymn a song sung to God
The children sang the hymn nicely.

Ii

ice water that is hard like stone, it is very cold
The sun has melted the ice.

icicle a thin pointed piece of ice. It hangs down from a roof or a tree
The icicles are hanging from the branches.

idea something you think of
It was a good idea to bring a drink with us.

idiot a very stupid person
She is behaving like an idiot.

ill feeling sick
After eating all the bananas John felt ill.

impossible something you cannot do
It is impossible for me to be home by eight o'clock.

improve make things better
A new carpet will improve this room.

include have someone in your group
We will include Rose in the team.

indoors inside a building
It started to rain. We ran indoors at once.

infant a baby
All the infants were crying.

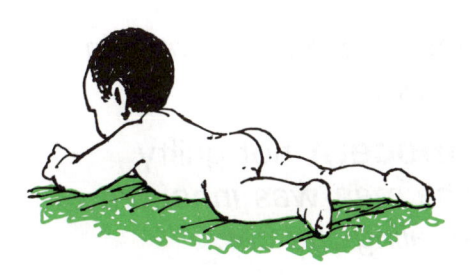

75

A a B b C c D d E e F f G g H h **I** i J j K k L l M m

infectious a sickness you can give to other people
Measles is a very infectious sickness.

inform tell someone something
The policeman informed us the road was closed.

initial the first letter of a name
The initial of my first name is J.

injection a way to put medicine into your body with a needle
The doctor gave me an injection against polio.

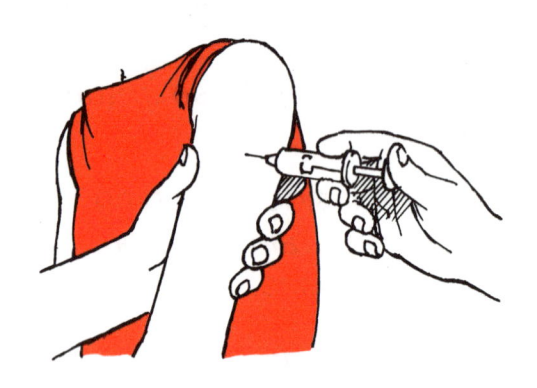

ink a coloured liquid, we use it for writing
She wrote her letters in black ink.

innocent not guilty
The man was innocent of stealing the car.

insect a small animal with six legs
Flies, ants, butterflies and bees are all insects.

inside in something, not outside it
There are six rooms inside that building.

interested want to find out about something
She is interested in singing.

invent think of and make something new
Alexander Graham Bell invented the telephone.

invisible cannot be seen
The plane was so high in the sky that it was invisible.

invite ask someone nicely to do something
Can I invite my friend to stay for the weekend?

N n O o P p Q q R r S s T t U u V v W w X x Y y Z z

iron 1 a heavy metal
The cooking pot was made of iron.
    2 a flat piece of metal with a handle, we use it to smooth clothes
Mother, please iron my shirt.

island a piece of land with water all around it
Madagascar is an island off the African coast.

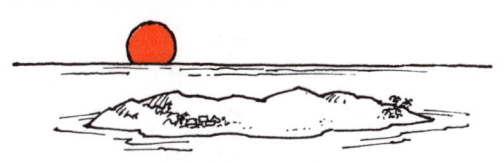

itch a tickling feeling on the skin
The dog scratched the itch on its back.

ivory the hard, white tusks of an elephant
Many elephants are killed for their ivory.

Jj

jackal a wild animal, it looks like a dog
The jackals waited until the lions had finished eating.

jacket a short coat
Sam wore his jacket to school.

jaguar a large, wild, spotted cat
Jaguars live in South America.

jam 1 a sweet food made by boiling sugar and fruit
I like bread and jam.
    2 caught in a crowd of people or cars, not able to move
The man missed the train because of the traffic jam.

January the first month of the year
January is named after the Greek god Janus.

77

A a B b C c D d E e F f G g H h I i **J j** K k L l M m

jar a glass or clay container
Mother made the jam. Then she put it into the jars.

jaw one of the bones that holds the teeth
The boxer hit him on the jaw.

jealous wanting something that someone else has
Ben was jealous because his brother had a new bicycle.

jelly a sweet food, it melts in your mouth
Jelly is made from fruit juice.

jersey clothes knitted in wool and worn on the top half of the body
Father is wearing his new jersey over his shirt.

jet 1 a liquid or gas coming very quickly out of a narrow opening
The jet of water shot up into the air.
2 a very fast aeroplane
The jet plane flew quickly across the sky.

jewel a valuable stone
Rubies, diamonds and pearls are all jewels.

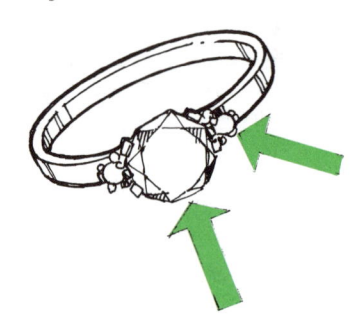

jewellery rings, brooches and jewels
I like jewellery. I want a diamond ring and a brooch.

jigsaw pieces of cardboard that fit together to make a picture
It took us all afternoon to do the jigsaw.

N n O o P p Q q R r S s T t U u V v W w X x Y y Z z

job the work you do for money
What is your father's job?

join 1 put two things together to make one thing
We joined the pieces of wood together with glue.
2 become part of a group
I am going to join the church choir.

joint the place where two things are fitted together
The ankle is the joint between the foot and the leg.

joke say or do something to make people laugh
Father is always telling jokes.

jolly happy
She is a very jolly person.

journey going from one place to another
It is a long journey to the nearest hospital.

joy happiness
He jumped with joy at the good news.

judge 1 a person who decides right and wrong
The judge sent the thief to prison.
2 decide what is best
You must judge the best cow.

juggler a person who throws and catches balls and plates
The juggler threw six plates in the air and caught them one by one.

juice the liquid in oranges and other fruit
He likes to drink pineapple juice.

July the seventh month of the year
July is a cold month in Zimbabwe.

A a B b C c D d E e F f G g H h I i **J j** K k L l M m

jump go over a low wall or a fence
The horse jumped over the wall.

June the sixth month of the year
My sister was born in June.

jungle the thick forests in hot countries
Monkeys live in the jungle.

junior younger
Primary schools are for junior children.

Kk

keep 1 have something which is yours
I keep my handkerchief in my pocket.
2 stay the same
Keep still! I want to take a photograph.
3 care for
My aunt keeps a cat and two dogs.

kennel a little house for a dog
I made a kennel for my new dog.

ketchup a sauce made with tomatoes
I like tomato ketchup with fish.

kettle a metal pot for boiling water
She boiled the kettle to make some tea.

key a piece of metal used for opening a lock
Use your key to open the car door.

kick hit with the foot
He kicked the ball into the goal.

N n O o P p Q q R r S s T t U u V v W w X x Y y Z z

kid a young goat
The kid played with the other goats in the field.

kidnap make a person a prisoner
The thieves kidnapped the rich man's child.

kill make a person or an animal die
The poacher killed the elephant with the rifle.

kilogram (kg) a measure, it tells how heavy things are
She bought five kilograms of maize.

kilometre (km) a measure, it tells how far things are
They live five kilometres from the town.

kind 1 good and helpful
She is kind to sick people.
    2 one type of thing
A Datsun is a kind of motor car.

king a man who rules a country
Shaka was the king of the Zulus.

kingfisher a bird with bright feathers, it lives near rivers
The kingfisher dived into the river to catch the fish.

kiss touch someone with your lips
The girl kissed her mother.

kitchen a room to cook food in
Mother is cooking food in the kitchen.

81

A a B b C c D d E e F f G g H h I i J j **K k** L l M m

kite 1 a paper toy, it flies in the wind
The wind blew the kite into the tree.

2 a bird of prey
The kite dived to catch the mouse in its beak.

kitten a young cat
The mother cat had six kittens.

knee the joint in the middle of your leg
He hurt his knee playing football.

knife a tool for cutting
He cut the meat with the knife.

knit use long needles and wool to make clothes
Mother used green wool to knit me a scarf.

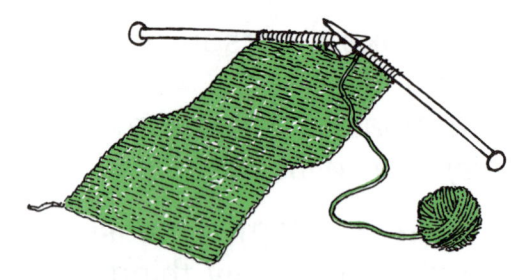

knock hit something hard
He knocked on the door very loudly.

knot the place where rope or ribbon is tied
She tied the green ribbon in a knot.

know 1 remember a person, a place or a thing
Do you know that man?
2 understand something
I know the way to make a kite.

knowledge all the things that you know
His knowledge of arithmetic is very good.

N n O o P p Q q R r S s T t U u V v W w X x Y y Z z

knuckle where the fingers join the hands
He hurt his knuckles hitting the door.

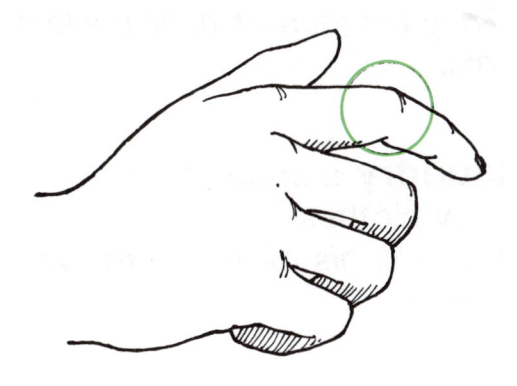

ladder wooden steps, they help you to reach higher places
He climbed the ladder to repair the roof.

lady another name for a woman
The kind lady gave us something to drink.

Ll

label the paper on a tin or bottle. It tells you what is in the bottle
The label on the tin said Baked Beans.

lace a piece of string to tie shoes
He broke his shoe lace.

lake a large piece of water, it has land all around it
The ferry took us across the lake.

lamb a young sheep
Lambs' wool is very soft.

A a B b C c D d E e F f G g H h I i J j K k **L l** M m

lame walk with a limp
She was lame for a long time after the accident.

lamp a light made by using a candle, oil or electricity
Light the lamp. It is getting dark.

land 1 the dry parts of the earth
The land here is covered with rocks.
2 come down to the ground, like a bird or an aeroplane
The plane landed at the airport.

lane a narrow road
They drove along the lane to the farm.

large very big
A mountain is larger than a hill.

last after everyone else
He came last in the race.

late after the right time
The train was two hours late.

laugh 1 make a sound to show that you are happy
The baby laughed happily in the cot.
2 show something is funny
They laughed at their uncle's joke.

laundry a shop to clean dirty clothes
He took his dirty suit to the laundry.

law the rules people must obey
Driving at 160 km an hour is against the law.

lawn the ground covered with grass in a garden
The children played with the ball on the lawn.

lay 1 place neatly
Help me lay the table.
2 make an egg
The hens lay eggs every day.

lazy not wanting to work
The lazy boy let his brother do all the work.

lead 1 a soft metal used to make pipes
The water pipes were made of lead.
2 go in front of
The guide will lead you around the museum.

leaf the green part of plants or trees
Only one leaf fell from the tree.

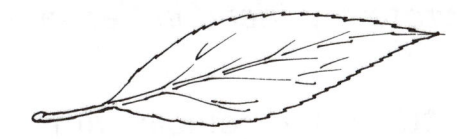

leak a small hole where air or water can escape
The water is leaking from that bucket.

lean 1 bend towards something
Do not lean out of that high window.
2 rest against something
He leaned the ladder against the wall.

learn find out things
Do you want to learn how to swim?

leather the material made from the skin of an animal
My mother bought a leather handbag.

leave 1 go away from a place
When are you leaving school?
2 not take something
I will leave you two bars of chocolate.

leek a long vegetable which tastes like an onion
Mother put leeks in the soup.

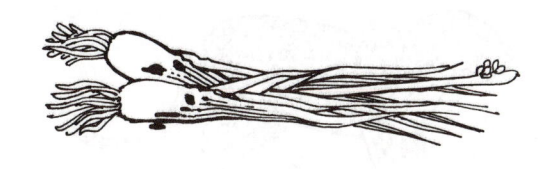

left the opposite of right
Hold the book in your left hand.

leg the part of your body that you walk and stand on
Lions have four legs. Humans have only two.

85

A a B b C c D d E e F f G g H h I i J j K k **L l** M m

lemon a yellow fruit with a sour taste
We have a lemon tree in our garden.

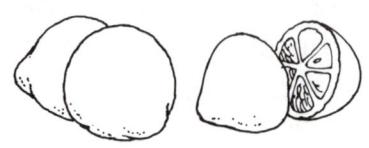

lend let someone have something for a time
I will lend you the book until tomorrow.

length how long something is
The road is five kilometres in length.

leopard a large, wild cat with yellow fur and black spots
It is hard to see leopards in the long grass.

less smaller than, not so much
They are arriving in less than an hour.

lesson the time when the teacher is teaching
We had a History lesson this morning.

let allow someone to do something
The teacher let them play football.

letter 1 signs like a, b, and c which are used to make words
A B C and D are all letters.
2 something you write to friends who are far away
I wrote my friend in Kenya a letter.

lettuce a vegetable with green leaves used in salads
Father grows lettuce, tomatoes and spinach.

level flat and smooth
The ground for the football field must be level.

liar a person who does not tell the truth
He said he did not steal the books. He is a liar. He did steal the books.

N n O o P p Q q R r S s T t U u V v W w X x Y y Z z

library a room with many books. People can take them to read
Mother took my books back to the library this morning.

lick touch with the tongue
The cow licked the calf all over.

lid a cover for a box or a pot
Put the lid back on the pot.

lie 1 say something not true
He is telling a lie. I did not break the cup.
　　2 flat on the ground or in bed
Lie down and rest on the bed.

life the time a person is alive
You are five years old. Your life has only started.

lift 1 pick up in your hand
The boy lifted the bag of maize easily.
　　2 a machine to take people up and down inside a high building
The lift took us up to the office on the tenth floor.

light 1 easy to carry, not heavy
Her father lifted her easily. She was as light as a feather.
　　2 start a fire
Please light the fire, it is very cold.

　　3 the brightness that lets you see
We can all see by the light of the sun.

87

A a B b C c D d E e F f G g H h I i J j K k **L l** M m

like 1 think someone or something is nice
I like oranges better than apples.
	2 nearly the same as
He looks just like his brother.

limp walk with a sore foot or leg, be lame
He limped off the field with a sore leg.

line 1 a long narrow mark like this _____

He drew a line across the page.
	2 a row of people
The soldiers stood in a straight line.

lion a large, fierce, African cat
The lion lay watching the herd of zebra.

lips the soft edges of the mouth
She licked her lips when she saw the chocolate cake.

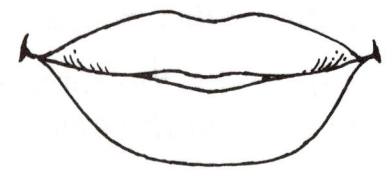

liquid things like water or milk
That white liquid is milk.

list the names of things or people written below each other
The teacher made a list of the boys' names.

listen try to hear something
Did you listen to the teacher in the English class?

litter 1 the rubbish people leave around
People drop litter in the streets. 
	2 baby animals born to a mother at one time
The sow had ten little pigs in her litter.

N n O o P p Q q R r S s T t U u V v W w X x Y y Z z

little very small
The small boy took a little piece of cake.

live 1 stay in your home
We live in a house in a big city.
　　　2 be alive
I hope to live for sixty or seventy years.

lizard an animal like a snake, it has legs
The lizard lay on the rock in the sun.

loaf a large piece of bread
Mother bought six loaves in the bakery.

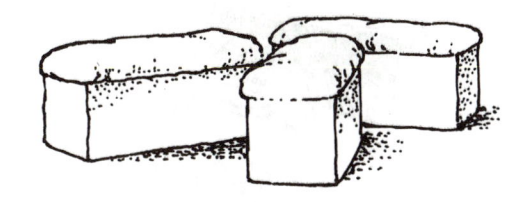

lock 1 close a door or box with a key
The teacher put the lock on the cupboard door.
　　　2 fasten firmly
The teacher locked the books in the cupboard.

log a piece of wood, it is cut from a tree
He put the logs on the fire.

lollipop a sweet on a stick
Children love to lick lollipops.

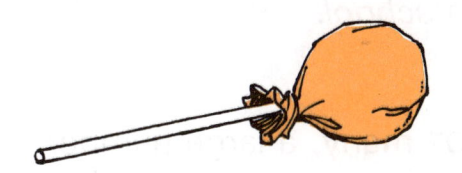

long a big distance or a lot of time
It's a long way to America, and it takes a long time to fly there.

look 1 use your eyes
Look! There is the bus.
　　　2 seem to be
Mother looks very tired.

loose not tied up
The bull escaped because the chain was loose.

lorry a large van, it carries things by road
They put all the boxes in the lorry.

89

A a B b C c D d E e F f G g H h I i J j K k **L l** M m

lose 1 beaten in a game
Did you lose the football match on Saturday?
2 cannot find something
She always loses her books in school.

lot many, a large number
There are a lot of children in the school.

loud noisy, easy to hear
Young people like loud music.

love like very much
David loves his sister.

lovely beautiful
Mother looked lovely in her new dress.

low not high
The lorry cannot go under that low bridge.

lunch the meal eaten in the middle of the day
She eats lunch at school.

Mm

machine a thing with a lot of parts that does a job
Father has bought a machine to cut the grass.

mad when your mind is sick
The mad dog bit the boy.

magazine a thin book, you can buy it every week or every month
Father gets his football magazine every month.

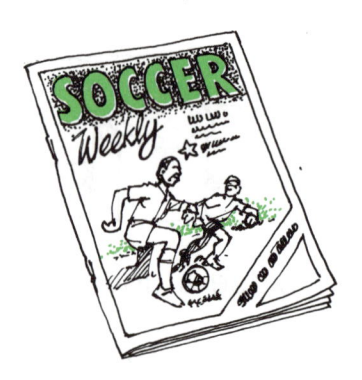

magic making strange things happen
The thief disappeared as if by magic.

N n O o P p Q q R r S s T t U u V v W w X x Y y Z z

magnet a piece of metal, it makes other pieces of metal stick to it
Mother picked the pins up with a magnet.

mail letters and parcels. They come in the post
I will pick up the mail at the post office today.

main the most important
This is the main road through town.

maize a plant with yellow seeds, we make flour and porridge from them
Maize is an important food in Africa.

make 1 put things together to get something new
John has made a boat out of wood and paper.
   2 get someone to do something
You made me go to bed early last night.

male any person or animal that can become a father
Men and bulls are both male.

mammal an animal that can feed its babies with its own milk
Whales, cows and dogs are mammals.

man a grown-up male person
The man lifted the little boy over the hole.

manners the way you act with other people
Mother has told us always to have good manners.

many a lot of
There are many elephants in Africa.

map a drawing, it shows the different places in the world
Can you find Nairobi on the map?

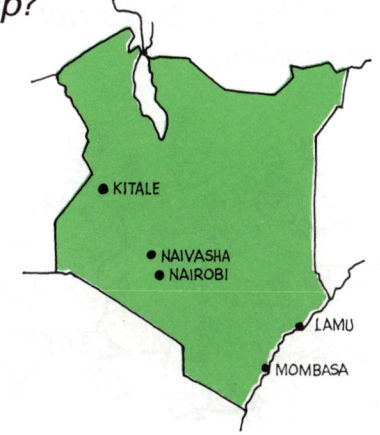

91

A a B b C c D d E e F f G g H h I i J j K k L l **M m**

March 1 the third month of the year
My uncle is coming to stay with us in March.

march 2 walk like a soldier
The soldiers marched down the street.

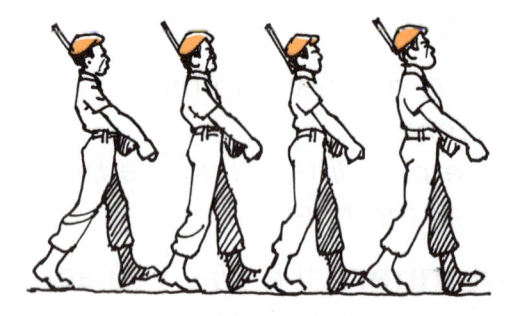

mark 1 a spot or a line on something
You have a dirty mark on your shirt.
2 show if a piece of schoolwork is good or bad
My sister got good marks in her English.

market a place where people buy and sell things
Mother always buys her fruit in the market.

marmalade a jam made from oranges or lemons
The oranges are cheap now. Mother is going to make marmalade.

marry become a husband or a wife
My sister is going to marry her boyfriend.

mask cloth or paper to cover the face
The man with the gun was wearing a mask.

mast a tall pole, it holds a ship's sail up
The mast broke and the ship's sail fell down.

N n O o P p Q q R r S s T t U u V v W w X x Y y Z z

master a man who tells people or animals what to do
The dog followed his master.

mat a small carpet
Mother has mats on the floor in winter.

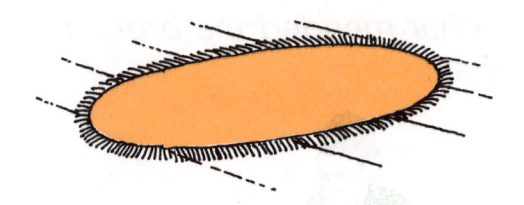

match 1 a game between two people or two teams
The football match will be played on Saturday.
2 a small, thin stick, you rub it against something rough to give a flame
I need a match to light the fire.

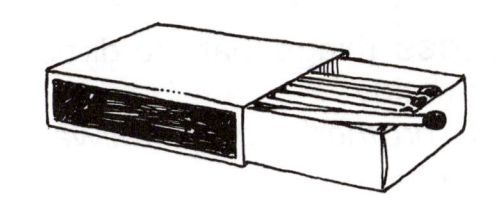

material 1 kinds of cloth
I will use the red material to make a dress.
2 something you use to make things
That material is leather. I use it to make shoes.

mathematics finding out about numbers and shapes
My father teaches Mathematics.

mattress the soft bag on a bed, you lie on it
They filled the mattresses with straw.

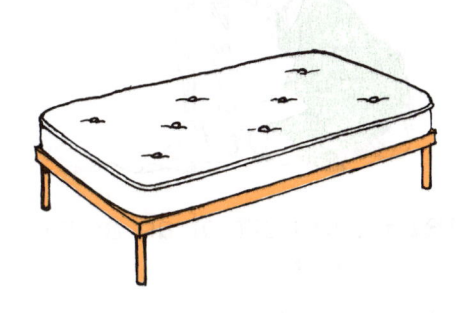

May 1 the fifth month of the year
June is the month after May.

may 2 it can happen
He may come today.

meal the food that you eat at the same time every day
We have our evening meal when father comes home.

measles a sickness. You have red spots on your skin and you are very hot
My brother is ill. He has measles.

A a B b C c D d E e F f G g H h I i J j K k L l **M m**

measure find out how big something is
Mother is measuring my brother. She is making him new trousers.

meat the part of an animal that we eat
I need two kilograms of meat for the stew.

medicine the pills or liquid that a sick person takes
My sister took her medicine. She soon felt better.

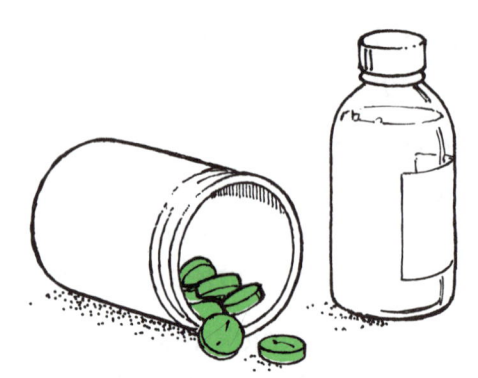

meet agree to see someone
I will meet you at the station.

memory remembering things
The old man has a good memory. He can remember the year the church was built.

mend fix something that was broken or damaged
Father mended the broken chair.

merry happy and laughing
The children walked down the road singing merrily.

mess things that are dirty or untidy
My brother's room is always in a mess.

94

N n O o P p Q q R r S s T t U u V v W w X x Y y Z z

message words that you send to someone when you cannot speak to him yourself
The teacher gave me a message to mother.

messenger a person who takes messages to people
The messenger took the letter to the post office.

metal something that is very hard but melts when it is heated
Gold, silver and iron are all metals.

metre a short measure of length, there are 1 000 metres in a kilometre
A very tall man could be two metres in height.

microphone an electric machine that makes your voice louder
The president used a microphone to speak to the crowd.

microscope a machine that makes things look bigger
The insect looked huge under the microscope.

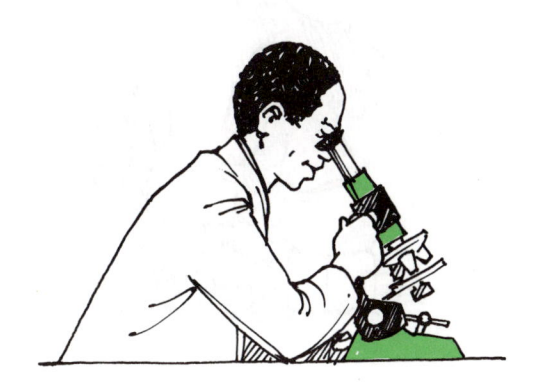

middle in the centre of a place
The children were playing in the middle of the field.

midnight twelve o'clock at night
I went to bed at midnight.

might 1 maybe do something
I might go to town tomorrow.
2 be allowed to do something
The teacher said I might go home.

95

A a B b C c D d E e F f G g H h I i J j K k L l **M m**

milk the white liquid from cows that we drink
I drink a litre of milk every day.

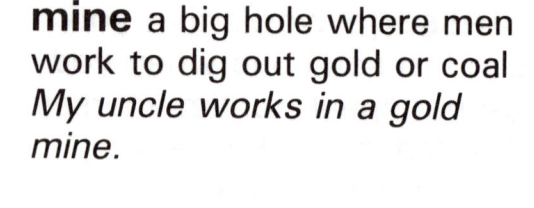

million the number 1 000 000 – a thousand thousands
I would love to have a million dollars.

mince cut up into very small pieces
Mother minces the meat to make stew.

mind 1 the part of your head that thinks and remembers
Everything you learn goes into your mind.
2 take care of something
I will mind the baby.

mine a big hole where men work to dig out gold or coal
My uncle works in a gold mine.

minute 1 sixty seconds
You have one minute to run round the garden.
2 a very short time
I will be with you in a minute.

mirror a piece of glass, you can see yourself in it
I can see my face in the mirror.

N n O o P p Q q R r S s T t U u V v W w X x Y y Z z

mischief doing silly or naughty things
The boys were told not to get into mischief when the teacher was away.

miss 1 fail to hit or catch something
I missed the bus and had to walk home.
2 be sad because someone has gone away
We will miss Uncle Joseph when he goes back to his village.

mist thin cloud which is near the ground
We could not see the trees because of the mist.

mistake something you have done that is wrong
There are six spelling mistakes in this sentence.

mix put different things together
Sally helped her mother mix the things for the cake.

mixture things mixed together
Purple is a mixture of red and blue.

modest not thinking of how good you are
My brother was modest about being first in the class.

Monday the second day of the week
Mother washes her clothes on Mondays.

money coins and notes used by people to buy and sell things
Father gives us money every week to buy sweets.

monkey a small animal with long arms and a long tail
The monkeys were swinging in the branches of the trees.

monster a big and frightening animal or something that is very large
The boys love to hear stories about monsters.

A a B b C c D d E e F f G g H h I i J j K k L l **M m**

month one of the twelve parts of the year
The baby is three months old.

moon a small planet that goes round the earth. We can see it in the sky at night
Sometimes the moon is round and sometimes it is like a part of a circle.

mop pieces of soft material on the end of a stick used for cleaning
Mother washed the floor with the mop.

more a larger number or a bigger amount
I would like some more stew.

morning the part of the day before noon
We leave for school at seven o'clock every morning.

moth an insect like a butterfly, it usually flies at night
Moths like to fly around lights at night.

mother a female parent
My mother has six children.

motor the part inside a machine or engine that makes it move
I need a new motor for the sewing machine. The old motor has stopped working.

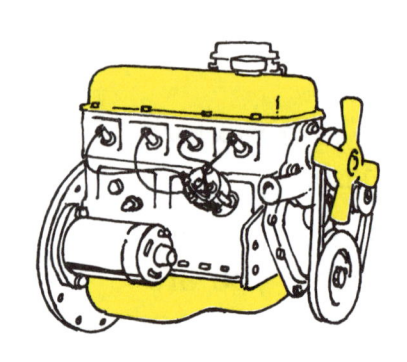

N n O o P p Q q R r S s T t U u V v W w X x Y y Z z

mountain a very high hill
Father likes to go climbing in the mountains.

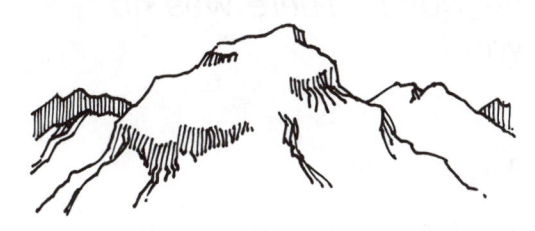

mouse a very small animal with a long tail and sharp teeth
The mouse chewed a hole in the kitchen door.

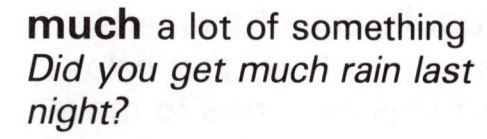

mouth a hole in the face, we use it for eating and speaking
The boy had too much food in his mouth. He could not speak.

move 1 go from one place to another
We are moving into our new house today.
   2 take something from one place to another
Please move that chair away from the window.

much a lot of something
Did you get much rain last night?

mud wet soil
The hippopotamus rolled in the mud.

mug a large cup for drinking
I would love a mug of coffee.

mule an animal that is half horse and half donkey
The mule pulled the cart slowly up the hill.

multiply make something bigger by a number of times
If you multiply twelve by three you get thirty-six.

A a B b C c D d E e F f G g H h I i J j K k L l **M m**

muscle one of the parts inside your body that helps your legs and arms to move
The runner had very strong muscles in his legs.

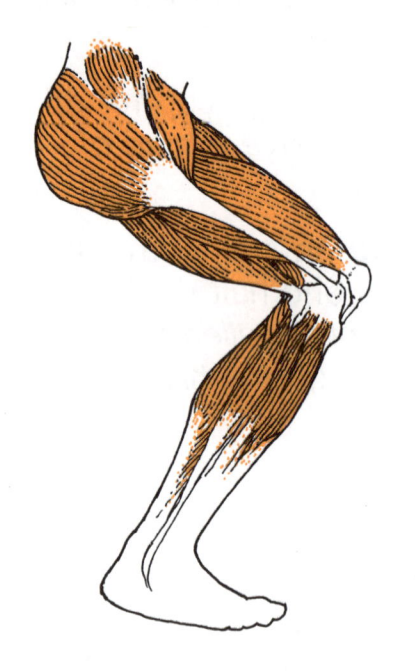

museum a place where interesting things are kept for people to go and see
Our class is going to the museum to see the old guns and spears.

music the sounds made by singing or playing the piano or violin
I would like to dance to this music.

must have to do something
You must get your hair cut today.

mystery something strange that has happened
It is a mystery why the tree fell down. There was no wind.

Nn

nail 1 the hard part that covers the ends of your fingers and toes
The baby needs her nails cut.
2 a small metal stick with a sharp point, used to fix pieces of wood together
I need some nails to fix the fence.

naked with no clothes on
The naked children played in the river.

N n O o P p Q q R r S s T t U u V v W w X x Y y Z z

name what you call a person, a place or thing
My name is Modise and I live in Botswana.

narrow not wide, thin
There was a narrow path between the houses.

nasty 1 not nice
What is that nasty smell?
2 very dirty
Who made that nasty mess on the floor?

nation a country and the people who live in it
The President spoke to the nation on the radio.

nature plants, animals, the sea, everything not made by people
The wild animals and the trees are all part of nature.

naughty acting badly
The teacher sent the naughty boy home from school.

navy 1 the warships of a country and the sailors who work in them
The ships of the French navy sailed out to sea.

2 dark blue
He was wearing a navy suit.

near not far away, close to
I live very near the school.

nearly almost
The bus nearly hit the car.

neat tidy
My clothes are always neat for school.

neck the part of the body between the head and shoulders
The giraffe has a very long neck.

101

A a B b C c D d E e F f G g H h I i J j K k L l M m

need have to do something
I have a sore foot, I need to go to the doctor.

needle a thin pointed piece of metal used for sewing or knitting
Sewing needles are small, knitting needles are much larger.

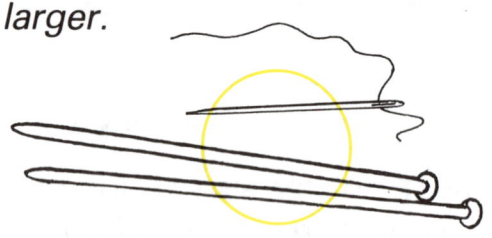

neither not this one and not that one
Neither mother nor father can drive a car.

nephew the son of a brother or sister
Uncle Joseph has two of his nephews living with him.

nervous easily frightened
Do not go near the horse. It is very nervous. It might kick you.

nest a home made by birds and some other animals
Mice make nests for their babies.

net pieces of string tied together to make a trap
The fisherman caught a lot of fish in his net.

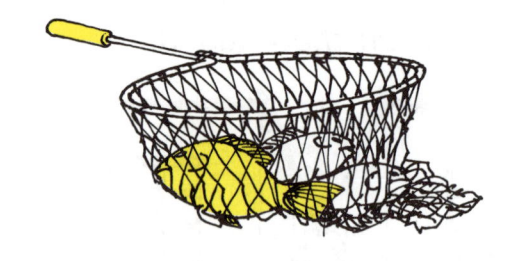

netball a team game. You throw a ball through a net to get a goal
My sister is very tall, she's good at netball.

never not even once
We never go to school on Sunday.

new something just bought or made
Mother bought us a new football.

news words telling you what is happening in different countries
Did you hear the news about the new baby?

next the time after this
I can't go this week, but I can go next week.

102

N n O o P p Q q R r S s T t U u V v W w X x Y y Z z

nib the point of a pen
Write carefully with that nib.

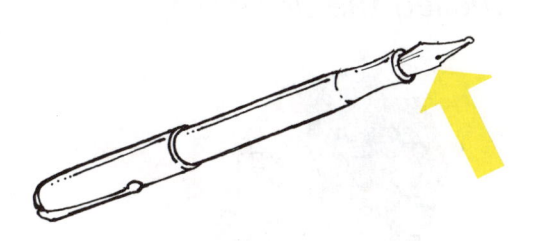

nine the number 9
That pig has nine little pigs.

nice kind or friendly
That nice boy helped me to carry the big box.

niece the daughter of your brother or sister
My brother has two daughters. They are my nieces.

night the part of the day when it is dark
I went to bed early last night.

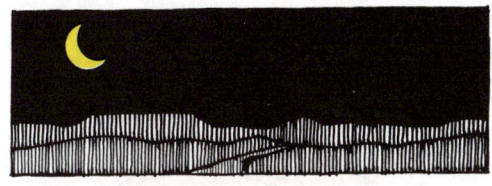

nightmare a frightening dream
My sister had a nightmare. She woke up crying.

nineteen the number 19
I have to milk nineteen cows every day.

ninety the number 90
There must be ninety elephants in that herd.

nip bite or squeeze with the fingers or teeth
The dog nipped me with its teeth.

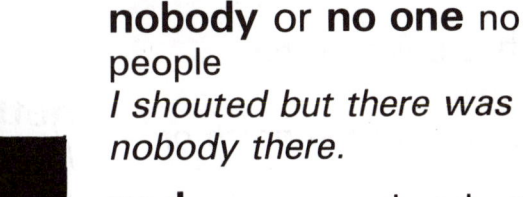

nobody or **no one** no people
I shouted but there was nobody there.

nod move your head up and down to show you agree
I saw him nod his head to say yes.

noise lots of loud sounds
The people watching the football match made a lot of noise.

103

A a B b C c D d E e F f G g H h I i J j K k L l M m

none not even one
I have five books. My brother has none.

nonsense speaking silly words
I don't understand. He is talking nonsense.

noon twelve o'clock in the daytime
The sun is high in the sky at noon.

north a point of the compass
Europe lies to the north of Africa.

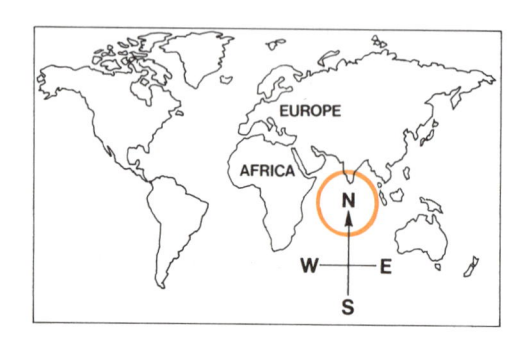

nose the part of your face used for smelling
The rabbit raised its nose. It smelled the dogs.

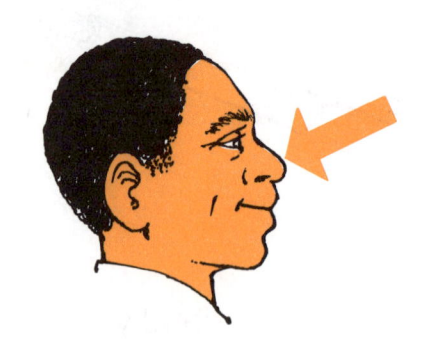

note 1 a short letter
Write a note to your uncle today.
      2 paper money
The man paid for the baskets with twenty dollar notes.

nothing not even one thing
I opened the box. There was nothing in it.

104

N n O o P p Q q R r S s T t U u V v W w X x Y y Z z

notice 1 see
He did not notice the ball on the stairs.
2 a paper with writing for everyone to read
The teacher put up the notice in the classroom.

noun a word which names a person, a place or a thing
The word Africa is a noun. It is the name of a place.

November the eleventh month of the year
November can be a rainy month.

now the present time
I want you to come with me now.

number words you use to count
1, 2, 3 and 4 are numbers.

nurse a person who cares for sick people
My mother works in the hospital. She is a nurse.

nut a hard fruit in a hard shell
Eat plenty of nuts. They are good for you.

Oo

oar a long piece of wood you use to row a boat
You row with one oar and I will row with the other.

oasis a place with water and trees in the desert
They were nearly dead when they found the oasis.

obedient always doing what you are told to do
My mother says the dog is very obedient.

obey do what you are told to do
A soldier should obey orders.

A a B b C c D d E e F f G g H h I i J j K k L l M m

object a thing you can see or touch
That shop is full of lovely objects.

ocean a big sea
The Pacific is a huge ocean.

o'clock the time on the clock
Look! It is four o'clock.

octagon a figure with eight sides
He has drawn an octagon in his book.

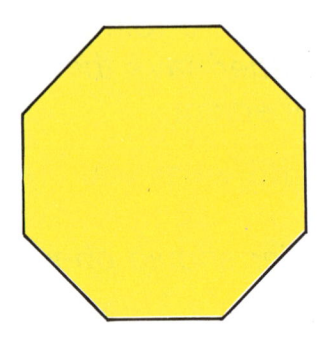

October the tenth month of the year
Her birthday is in October.

octopus a sea animal with eight long arms
The octopus caught the fish in its arms.

odd 1 strange, not normal
He looks odd in that huge hat.
　　2 numbers which cannot be divided by two
1, 3, 5 and 7 are all odd numbers.

offer say you are willing to do something
I will offer to take the children home.

office a room where business people work
Mary is a typist. She works in an office.

N n **O o** P p Q q R r S s T t U u V v W w X x Y y Z z

officer a person in the army or navy who gives orders
The officer told the soldiers to stand still.

often lots of times
I often play football with my father.

oh a cry, it can be happy or surprised
Oh, thank you. I really want to go to your party.

oil 1 a thick liquid used to make machines run well
I oil my bicycle every week.

2 a kind of oil is also used in cooking
They roasted the meat in cooking oil.

old born or made a long time ago
Look at that strange car. It must be very old.

once only one time
My father saw the chief once a long time ago.

one the number 1
I have one father and one mother.

onion a round, white vegetable with a strong taste and strong smell
Cutting onions always makes me cry.

only 1 one person or thing
She is the only child in that family.

2 not more than
There are only three apples.

open not shut
Please open the door. I want to go home.

opposite 1 on the other side
His house is on the opposite side of the road.

2 as different as a thing can be
Hot is the opposite of cold.

107

A a B b C c D d E e F f G g H h I i J j K k L l M m

orange 1 a round juicy fruit
They made a cold drink from the oranges.

2 the colour of the fruit, the same colour as a carrot
Mother was wearing an orange dress.

orbit the path of a planet round the sun or a rocket round the earth
The earth orbits the sun once a year.

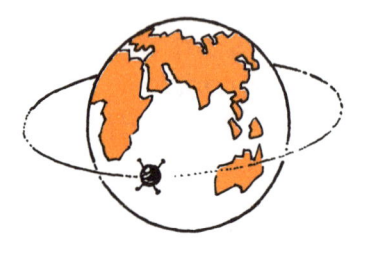

orchard a field with fruit trees in it
The boys stole the oranges from the orchard.

orchestra a group of people who play music together
My brother plays the violin in the orchestra.

order tell someone to do something
The pupil cannot order the teacher to help.

ordinary just like other people or other things
They are an ordinary family.

N n **O o** P p Q q R r S s T t U u V v W w X x Y y Z z

orphan a boy or girl without a father or a mother
She is an orphan. Her parents were killed in an accident.

ostrich a big bird with long legs and beautiful tail feathers
Ostriches are birds that cannot fly.

other the second of two things
Don't take this book, take the other.

otter a furry animal that lives near water
Otters have long tails and they love to play in the water.

out not in the house
I came to your house but you were out.

outside in the open air
Let's go outside. It's very warm in the house.

oval a shape like an egg
The runners run round an oval track.

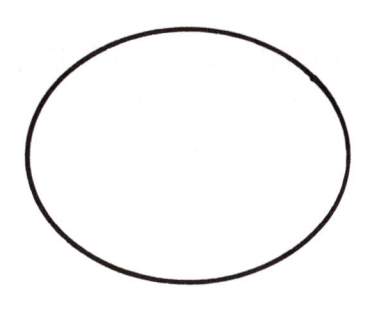

oven the closed part of a cooking stove
Mother cooked the chicken in the oven.

109

A a B b C c D d E e F f G g H h I i J j K k L l M m

over 1 finished
The birthday party was soon over.
    2 from one side to the other
The boys climbed over the fence.

owe have to pay money to someone
They owe me a lot of money.

owl a large bird with big eyes, it hunts at night
The owl was able to see the mouse in the dark.

own have something which belongs to you
He owns forty cows and sixty goats.

ox large cattle used to pull carts
The farmer used his ox to plough the field.

oyster a fish which lives in a shell
Try to open the shell of that oyster. You might find a pearl in it.

Pp

pace one step
It was ten paces to the tree.

pack 1 put things into a case or box
I will pack the clothes in the case.
    2 a group of dogs or other animals
A pack of dogs chased the goats.

paddle 1 a long, flat piece of wood used to make a canoe move
The boy paddled the canoe across the river.

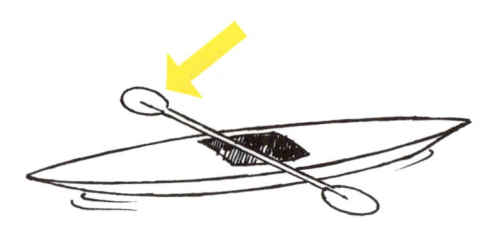

N n O o **P p** Q q R r S s T t U u V v W w X x Y y Z z

2 walk in shallow water
Mother said we could paddle in the river.

page a piece of paper, a part of a book
This book has fifty pages.

pain the feeling you have when you are sick or hurt
Mother gave me medicine for the pain in my head.

paint 1 a coloured liquid put on walls to make them nice
I will paint that wall blue.
2 put the liquid on a wall
Father is going to paint the house blue.

pair two things that go together
I need a new pair of shoes.

palace a big house where a king or queen lives
There were sixty bedrooms in the palace.

pale not bright
The sky is pale blue today.

palm 1 the inside of the hand
He caught the ball in the palm of his hand.

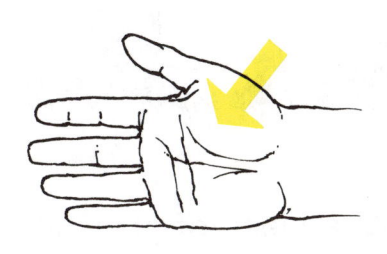

2 a tree that grows in hot countries
Dates grow on palm trees.

111

A a B b C c D d E e F f G g H h I i J j K k L l M m

pan a flat pot for cooking
Mother cooked the chicken in the pan.

panda a large black and white animal that looks like a bear
Pandas live in China.

pane a piece of glass in a window or door
He threw the ball and broke the window pane.

pant breathe quickly
The man was panting after chasing the robber.

pants another name for trousers
The boy wore brown pants and a red shirt.

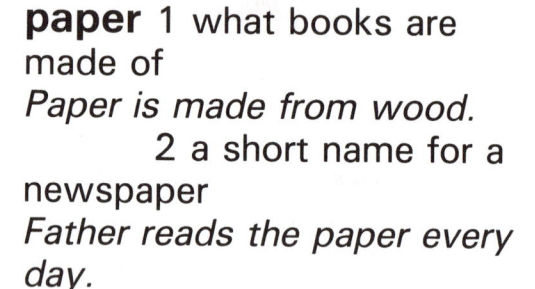

paper 1 what books are made of
Paper is made from wood.
2 a short name for a newspaper
Father reads the paper every day.

parachute a large cloth for floating to earth from an aeroplane
The man jumped from the plane and his parachute opened at once.

N n O o **P p** Q q R r S s T t U u V v W w X x Y y Z z

parcel something wrapped in paper and tied with string
The parcel arrived in the post this morning.

parent a mother or father
His parents loved their son very much.

park a place with grass and trees, people can walk or play there
The park was full of children playing games.

parrot a large bird with bright feathers
Some parrots can copy human words.

part a bit of something bigger
A wheel is a part of a bicycle.

party a group of people having fun together
I am going to a birthday party this week.

pass 1 give something to another person
Pass me the salt, please.
2 kick or throw a ball to another person
I am going to pass the ball to the goalkeeper.

passenger a person in a car or a bus or a train with a driver
There were forty passengers in the bus.

past any time before the present
In the past we had no radio or television.

paste a liquid for sticking paper
We made some paste to stick the pictures in our books.

113

A a B b C c D d E e F f G g H h I i J j K k L l M m

pastry flour and water mixed together and cooked
My mother makes pies with pastry.

pat hit very gently
Pat the dog. Then you will be friends.

patch a piece of cloth used to cover a hole in your clothes
My mother put a patch on my old trousers.

path a narrow road for walking
Take that path to walk into the village.

patient 1 a sick person who goes to a doctor
There are fifty patients in that hospital.
2 willing to wait quietly
He is a patient person. He waited for two hours.

paw the foot of an animal
The dog is crying. He has hurt his paw.

pay give money to buy something
I will pay for the book with my own money.

pea a little, round, green vegetable
I like to eat peas and potatoes.

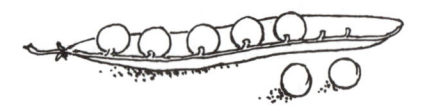

peace a quiet time when there is no war
There will be peace in South Africa one day.

peach a juicy, yellow fruit with a hard stone
My mother loves to eat peaches.

peacock a large bird with long tail feathers
Look! That peacock is showing his feathers.

114

N n O o **P p** Q q R r S s T t U u V v W w X x Y y Z z

pear a long juicy fruit
I like pears better than apples.

pearl a white jewel found in oysters
Do you know that pearls grow inside oysters?

pebble a small smooth stone
Don't throw that pebble! You can hurt someone.

pedal 1 the part of a bicycle you push with your foot
This bicycle is too big. I cannot use the pedals.

2 turn the pedals of a bicycle
I pedal my bicycle to school every day.

peel take the skin off fruit
I can peel an orange with my fingers.

pelican a big bird with a large beak to carry fish
Pelicans look very strange with their huge beaks.

pen 1 a stick with a metal point used for writing with ink
I write my letters with my pen.

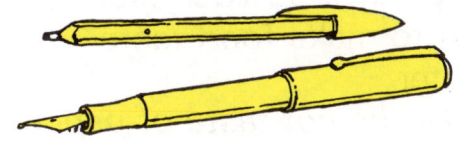

2 a place with a fence round it to keep animals in
We put the goats in a pen at night.

115

A a B b C c D d E e F f G g H h I i J j K k L l M m

pencil a wooden stick used for writing and drawing
Can I use your pencil to draw a house?

penknife a small knife you can carry in your pocket
Cut the paper with your penknife.

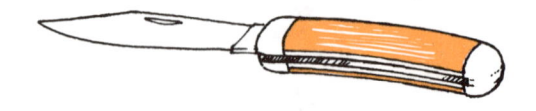

people men and women and children
All the people came to see the football team.

pepper a powder used with salt to make food taste better
I like the hot taste of pepper on my meat.

perch 1 a fish which lives in lakes and rivers
I caught four perch in the river this morning.

2 a stick for birds to stand on
All the hens were standing on the perch.

perfect very good, cannot be better
I washed the car. It looks perfect.

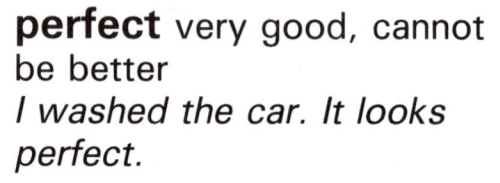

person a man or a woman or a child
The person who owns this car must move it immediately.

pet an animal kept as a friend
I have a pet mouse. Do you have a pet?

petal the coloured parts of a flower
The wind has blown all the petals from the flower.

116

N n O o **P p** Q q R r S s T t U u V v W w X x Y y Z z

petrol the liquid put in car engines to make them go
I will put some petrol in the car today.

photograph a picture taken with a camera
He took a photograph of the family.

piano a machine for playing music
She played the piano in school every day.

pick choose one thing from many
Pick the biggest orange.

picnic a meal you eat outside
We are going for a picnic tomorrow.

picture a painting or a drawing or a photograph
He has drawn a picture of a camel.

pie a food made with meat or fruit covered with pastry
I love chicken pie for dinner.

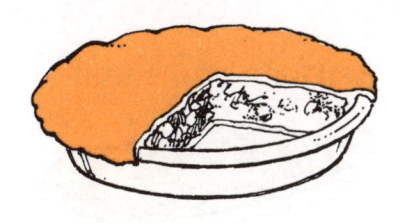

piece a part of something
I will eat two pieces of cake.

pig a fat animal with short legs. Farmers keep them for meat
The pig was lying in the mud.

pigeon a grey bird
There are lots of pigeons on the roof.

pill a small, hard piece of medicine
My mother gives me two pills every morning.

117

A a B b C c D d E e F f G g H h I i J j K k L l M m

pillow a bag full of feathers to put your head on in bed
I have a soft pillow in my bed.

pin a small piece of metal with a sharp point
The pin will hold the papers together.

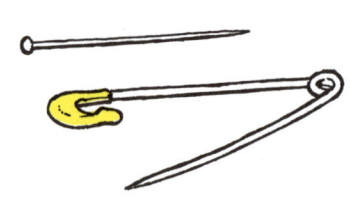

pinch nip with a finger and thumb
I pinched his leg to waken him.

pink a pale red colour
I am wearing a pink dress and my sister is wearing a blue one.

pip the seed of an orange or an apple
Don't eat the orange pips. Throw them away.

pipe a tube to take water from place to place
That pipe brings water to the house.

place where you put something
This is the place where I put the box.

plain ordinary, without a lot of colour
He wore a plain white shirt.

plane a name for an aeroplane
He is going to London by plane.

planet a world that goes round the sun
Earth is one of the planets.

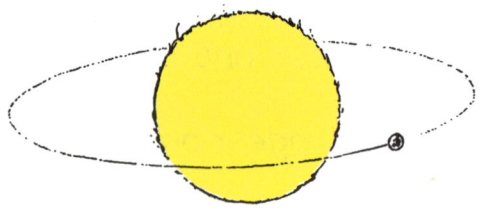

plant 1 anything that grows in the ground
Trees, bushes and flowers are all plants.
2 put seeds or roots in the ground to grow
I planted those flowers last year.

118

N n O o **P p** Q q R r S s T t U u V v W w X x Y y Z z

plastic a strong material used to make all kinds of things
I want plastic cups, plastic saucers and plastic dishes, please.

plate a flat dish to put food on
Put all the meat on that plate.

play 1 take part in a game or a sport
I play netball with my sister every day.
2 a story that you act
My sister and I took part in the school play.

please a word we use to ask for things in a nice way
Can I have another piece of cake, please?

plenty lots of something
There is plenty of food for everyone.

plough a machine for digging the soil on farms
The horse pulls the plough for my father.

plug a thing used to fill a hole
Put the plug in the bath before you turn on the tap.

pocket a small bag in your trousers or skirt
I keep my money in my pocket.

poem a piece of writing, to tell a story or to describe something
I wrote a poem about our house.

119

A a B b C c D d E e F f G g H h I i J j K k L l M m

point 1 the sharp tip on a pin or needle
An arrow has a sharp point.

2 use your finger or a stick to show something
'I live there.' He pointed to a white house.

poison a powder or a liquid that can kill
Don't drink from that bottle. It might be poison.

pole a long stick
There is a flag at the top of that pole.

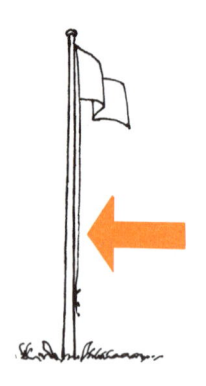

police men and women who stop people from doing bad things
The police caught the thief in our house.

pond a very small lake
The ducks swim in the pond.

pony a small horse
My young sister rides a pony.

pool a small piece of water
The fish swim in a pool in the river.

poor have no money
I have no clothes or shoes. I am very poor.

pop a very small bang
The balloon burst with a pop.

popular liked by a lot of people
Football is very popular here.

porridge a food made of maize boiled in water
I love porridge for breakfast.

N n O o **P p** Q q R r S s T t U u V v W w X x Y y Z z

port a town with a harbour
Mombasa is a large port in Kenya.

possible something you can do
It is possible for us to swim across that river.

post 1 a long, thick stick
The posts in our fence are broken.
2 send a letter
Please post these letters for me.

pot a container made of dry clay or metal
Those clay pots are beautiful.

potato a round, white vegetable with a brown skin
I like a potato with my dinner.

pour put a liquid from one container into another
Pour the milk into the cups. I will pour the tea.

powder very small pieces, like flour
The powder is in my nose. I am going to sneeze.

power something to make machines and engines go
The power that makes the lights work is electricity.

practise work hard to do something letter
We practise football every week.

prayer words to ask God to help you
I say a prayer every night before bed.

present 1 now, today
At present the school is on holiday.
2 something a person gives you
I got four presents for my birthday.

press squeeze or push
Press the button to ring the bell.

pretty nice to look at
She has a very pretty face.

121

A a B b C c D d E e F f G g H h I i J j K k L l M m

price the money you pay for something
I cannot buy the book. The price is too high.

pride a group of lions
The pride of lions killed the antelope.

primary first
Primary school is the first school you go to.

prince the son of a king
He is a prince from an African country. His father is king.

print put words on a page using a machine
We can print the pages of a book on a machine.

prison a place where the police keep bad people
The police put the thief in prison.

prize something you get for winning
The first prize is a bicycle.

promise say you will do something
I promise to work hard.

pudding a food you eat after the meat and vegetables
Mother makes a nice pudding on Sundays.

puddle a small pool of water
It is raining. Look at all the puddles.

puff take short breaths
I always puff when I am running.

puff-adder a fat poisonous snake
A puff-adder is very dangerous.

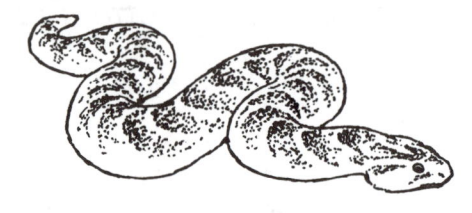

pull bring something towards you
My father pulled the big box into the house.

pump a machine to move liquids in pipes
The pump brings the water to the house.

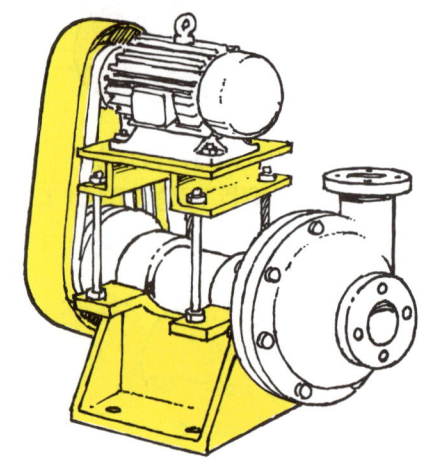

N n O o **P p** Q q R r S s T t U u V v W w X x Y y Z z

punch hit with your fist
Don't punch him in the face.

puncture a hole in a tyre
The piece of glass put a puncture in my bicycle tyre.

pupil a boy or girl in school
The pupils in this class are all very good.

puppet a doll, the head, legs and arms can move
That puppet looks alive.

puppy a young dog
The dog has three lovely puppies.

purr make the sound a happy cat makes
Stroke the cat and it will start to purr.

purse a small bag to keep money in
My sister keeps all her money in her purse.

push move something in front of you
My bicycle has a puncture. I will push it home.

put place something
I put all the pieces of paper in the fire.

puzzle a game or question to make you think hard
In this puzzle you pick the right pictures.

pygmy a very small person or animal
The pygmy hippopotamus is very small.

pyjamas the clothes you wear in bed
I wear my blue pyjamas in bed every night.

pyramid a solid shape with a square bottom and sides like triangles
There are big pyramids in Egypt.

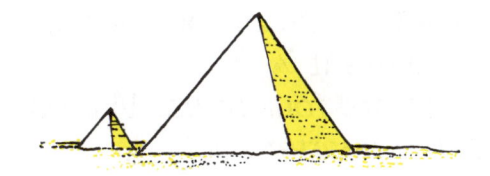

123

python a very big snake. It squeezes small animals to kill them
Look! That python must be six metres long.

quay a place where boats are tied up
They are putting the boxes on the boat at the quay.

queen the wife or mother of a king, or a woman ruler
The queen sat beside the young princess while the king spoke to the soldiers.

Qq

quarrel be angry with someone who does not agree with you
They quarrelled over the right way to go.

quarry a place where people dig stone out of the ground
They got those big pieces of stone from the quarry.

quarter one of four parts, you write it ¼
There are four of us. We can take a quarter each.

queer strange
Listen! What is that queer noise?

question something you ask to get an answer
Here is a question. What is the capital of Kenya?

N n O o P p **Q q** R r S s T t U u V v W w X x Y y Z z

queue people waiting in a line
There is a queue outside the new shop.

quick fast
Be quick. Those big boys are chasing us.

quiet not noisy, silent
The house was quiet. There was no one there.

quiz a game of answering questions
The teacher has a Geography quiz every Friday. My sister won this week.

Rr

rabbit a small furry animal with long ears
Rabbits live in holes in the ground.

race find out who is the fastest runner
I will race you to the classroom.

racket a kind of bat with strings
He hit the ball hard with his racket.

radio a machine that brings voices and music from a great distance
I listen to the radio every day.

radius a straight line from the centre of a circle to the edge
This circle has a radius of six centimetres.

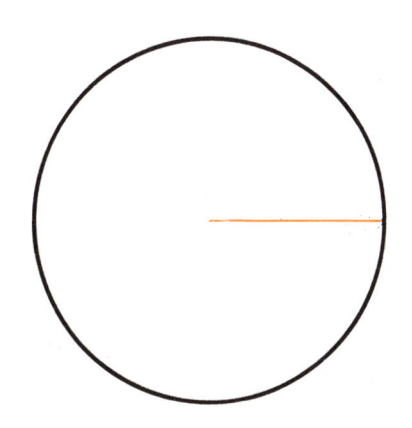

A a B b C c D d E e F f G g H h I i J j K k L l M m

raft pieces of wood tied together to make a boat
The boys sailed across the river on the raft.

rag an old piece of cloth
Father wiped his dirty hands on a rag.

rage great anger
The teacher was in a rage. He was so angry he could not speak.

rail a long metal rod
Trains run on rails.

rain drops of water that fall from clouds
We need rain to make the corn grow.

rainbow lines of bright colours that you see in the sky
When the sun shines through the rain you can see a rainbow.

raise lift up
Will you help me to raise this heavy stone?

raisin a dried grape
Mother put some raisins in the cake.

rake a tool that you use in the garden
Give me the rake. I will clear up the leaves.

ram a male sheep
Rams have large horns.

ranch a large cattle farm
My uncle has a ranch near here.

rap knock quickly
The policeman rapped loudly on the door.

rapid very quick
The firemen moved rapidly into the burning house.

rare not often found
The panda is a rare animal.

N n O o P p Q q **R r** S s T t U u V v W w X x Y y Z z

rascal a naughty child
Mother says my brother is a rascal because he disobeys her.

rash red spots on the skin
The doctor gave her pills for her rash.

rat an animal like a large mouse
The rat was in the bin eating the corn.

rattle make a sound by shaking stones in a tin
Shake those stones in that tin. They will rattle.

raven a large black bird
Ravens are very noisy birds.

raw not cooked
I like to eat raw carrots.

ray a thin line of light
The sun's rays came through the window.

reach 1 put out your hand
Father reached for a piece of cake.
2 arrive at a place
When we reach home we will have a cup of tea.

read understand words that are written down
I like to read adventure books.

ready able to do something now
We are ready to go to the cinema.

real not a copy, true
Are those real flowers in that vase?

rear the back part of something
The baby donkey walked at the rear of the herd.

reason why you do or say a thing
The reason I am late is because my car broke down.

receive take something you are given
He received the prize for his good work.

127

A a B b C c D d E e F f G g H h I i J j K k L l M m

recipe words to tell you how to cook food
I have a recipe for apple cake.

recognise remember someone because you have seen them before
The farmer recognised the man who had stolen his cattle.

record a round, flat piece of black plastic, we play it on a record player to hear music
This record makes me want to dance.

rectangle a shape with four straight sides
A football field is the shape of a rectangle.

red the colour of blood
My sister is wearing a red dress.

referee a person who makes sure that players obey the rules
The referee sent the player off for fighting.

reflection a picture that you see in a mirror or in water
You can see the reflection of the trees in the water.

refrigerator a large metal box that keeps food and drink cold
Mother put the milk in the refrigerator.

reign 1 be a king or a queen
The king has reigned for twenty years.
    2 the time when someone is king or queen
America was discovered during the reign of Queen Elizabeth 1.

N n O o P p Q q **R r** S s T t U u V v W w X x Y y Z z

reins two long pieces of leather, they tell a horse which way to go
Do not pull the reins hard. You will hurt the horse's mouth.

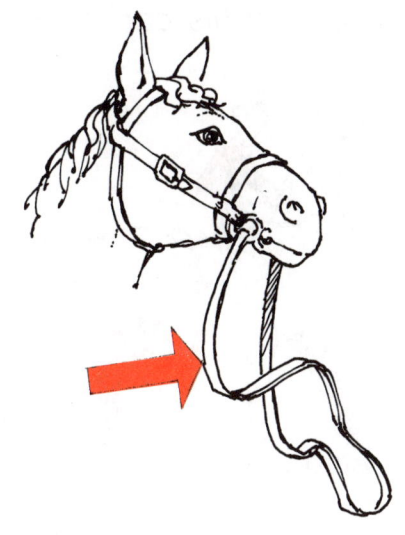

relative someone in your family
Only our relatives are coming to the party.

remember keep something in your mind
I must remember to lock the door.

remove take something away
Please remove your goats from my field.

reptile an animal that crawls along the ground
Snakes, lizards and crocodiles are all reptiles.

rescue save someone from danger
The policeman rescued the girl from the burning house.

rest 1 sit down and be quiet
The dog rested under the tree.
     2 the bit that is left
Mother put the rest of the cake in a big tin.

result what happens in the end
The accident was the result of bad driving.

reward a present. You give it to someone because he has done something good
Joe got a reward for putting out the fire.

rhinoceros a large heavy animal with thick skin
Rhinoceroses have horns on their noses.

rhyme words that have the same sounds at the end
Cat and mat rhyme.

129

A a B b C c D d E e F f G g H h I i J j K k L l M m

rib one of the bones in your chest
He fell off the roof. He broke one of his ribs.

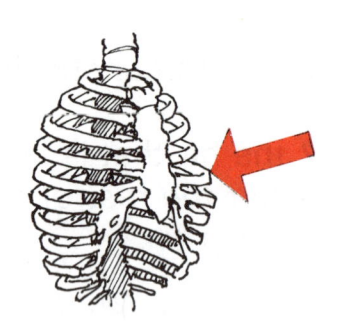

ribbon a narrow piece of material
She wore a red ribbon in her hair.

rice a thin plant, we eat the white seeds from it
Rice grows in hot, wet places.

rich have a lot of money
The rich man lived in a large house.

ride 1 sit on a horse or bicycle as it moves along
I can ride a bicycle.
       2 travel in a car, bus or train
Father will give us a ride to the shops in his car.

rifle a long gun
The man raised the rifle to his shoulder. He shot at the lion.

right 1 not wrong, correct
That is the right way to play netball.
        2 the opposite of left
Most people write with their right hand.

130

N n O o P p Q q **R r** S s T t U u V v W w X x Y y Z z

ring 1 a circle of thin metal, we wear it on a finger
Mother wears a gold ring on her finger.

2 make a sound like a bell
The church bell rings every Sunday.

rinse wash in clean water
I will rinse the shirts in the basin

rip tear
The dog ripped the boy's pants with its teeth.

ripe ready to be picked or eaten
The bananas are ripe enough to eat.

rise go up
The sun rises at the same time every day.

river the water that flows into the sea or a lake
There are many fish in the river.

road a wide track that people, cars and animals use to go on a journey
They are building a new road to the next village.

roar a loud, deep noise
We could hear the roar of the lions.

roast cook meat inside an oven, or over a fire
Mother is roasting meat in the oven for dinner.

rob steal things from people
He robbed me of all my money.

robe a long coat
Judges wear robes.

131

A a B b C c D d E e F f G g H h I i J j K k L l M m

robot a machine, it does some of the jobs people do
Many cars are now made by robots.

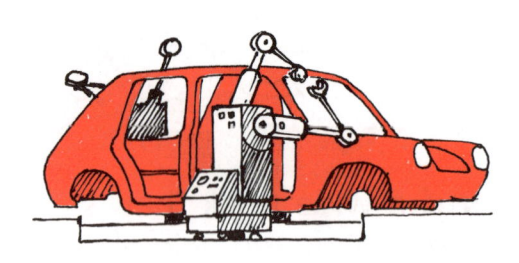

rock 1 a big stone
A large rock rolled down the mountain.
   2 move from side to side
She rocked the baby to stop it from crying.

rocket a tall metal tube that is shot into space
This rocket is going to the moon.

rod a long, thin piece of wood or metal
The boy tied a piece of string on to the end of his rod and sat by the river to fish.

roll 1 a long tube
I would like that roll of material please.
   2 a very small loaf of bread
My sister takes a jam roll for her lunch.
   3 turn over like a ball
He rolled all the way down the hill.

roof the top part of a building
We put a new roof on the house.

N n O o P p Q q **R r** S s T t U u V v W w X x Y y Z z

rooster a male fowl
Roosters make a lot of noise in the morning.

rope very thick string
He tied the boxes with a rope.

room 1 one of the parts of a house
Kitchens and bedrooms are all rooms.
2 space for someone or something
Is there any room left on the bus?

root the part of the plant that grows under the soil
Some plants have roots that you can eat.

rot go bad
This fruit is starting to rot. We cannot eat it.

rough 1 not smooth or flat
This wood is too rough to make a nice table.
2 not gentle
Do not play with that boy. He is very rough.

round shaped like a circle
We have a round table in the kitchen.

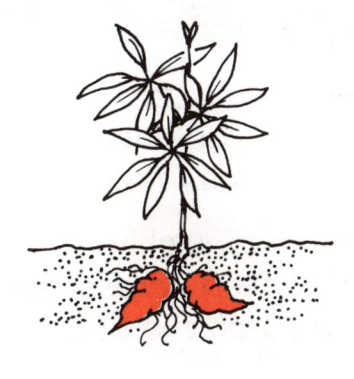

A a B b C c D d E e F f G g H h I i J j K k L l M m

row 1 a line of people or things
The children all sat in rows.
2 a loud quarrel
Stop that row! You will waken the children.
3 make a boat move with oars
Eight men row this big boat.

rub keep moving your hand or a cloth against something
My mother rubbed cream into my face.

rubber a strong material, we make tyres with it
Rubber comes from the rubber tree.

rubbish things that you do not want
The men come every Tuesday to collect the rubbish.

ruby a red jewel
She had three rubies in her brooch.

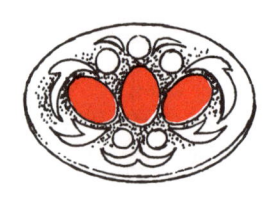

rude have bad manners
She spoke rudely to her father.

rug a kind of mat
The dog is on the rug in front of the door.

rule something people must obey
You must come to school on time. That is a rule.

ruler 1 the leader of a country
Daniel Arap Moi is the ruler of Kenya.
2 a piece of wood or plastic to make straight lines
I took my ruler to school with me.

run move your legs quickly
Can you run as fast as I can?

rush move quickly
We all rushed across the road to catch the bus.

N n O o P p Q q **R r** S s T t U u V v W w X x Y y Z z

rust a brown stain on damp metal
The bridge over the river was brown with rust.

Ss

sack 1 a large strong bag
The men put the potatoes into sacks.

2 stop someone working at a job
He got the sack. He was always late for work.

sad not happy
We were sad when the old man died.

safe 1 a strong metal box
The lady kept her money and jewels in the safe.
2 free from danger
Stay in the house and you will be safe.

sail 1 travel on water
It will take us two days to sail across the lake.
2 a large piece of cloth tied to the mast of a ship
The sails filled with wind and the ship began to move quickly.

sailor a man who works on a ship
There are one hundred sailors on that ship.

saint a very good person
He looks after the poor children. He is a saint.

salad a mixture of raw vegetables
Mother cut up the vegetables for the salad.

salt a white powder, we use it on food for a nice taste
Mother put salt and pepper on the table.

same not different
My twin sister and I are the same age.

sand very small pieces of rock
You find sand in the desert and beside the sea.

135

A a B b C c D d E e F f G g H h I i J j K k L l M m

sandal a shoe made with thin pieces of leather.
Sandals are cool in hot weather.

sandwich two pieces of bread with food between them
Father takes meat sandwiches to work.

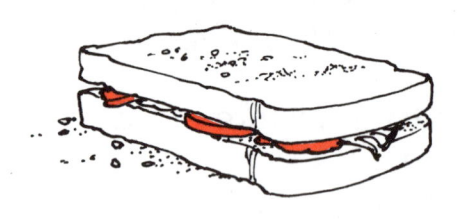

sardine a small fish
Sardines are usually sold in tins.

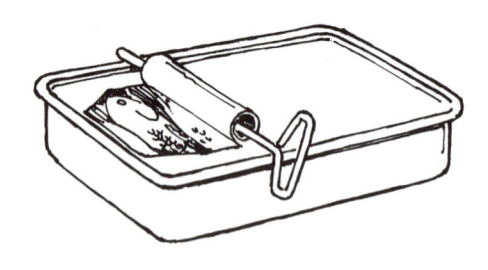

Saturday the last day of the week
We do not go to school on Saturday.

sauce a thick liquid that you put on food
This cheese sauce is very good with rice.

saucepan a metal cooking pot
She cooked the porridge in the saucepan.

save 1 keep something so it can be used later
I am saving my money to buy a radio.
2 rescue someone or something
He saved her from the angry bull.

saw a tool to cut wood
Mike cut the tree down with his saw.

N n O o P p Q q R r **S s** T t U u V v W w X x Y y Z z

say make words with your mouth and voice
He says that he did not steal the book.

scales 1 a machine for weighing things
Use the scales to weigh the meat.

2 thin pieces of skin on a fish
Fish and snakes have scales.

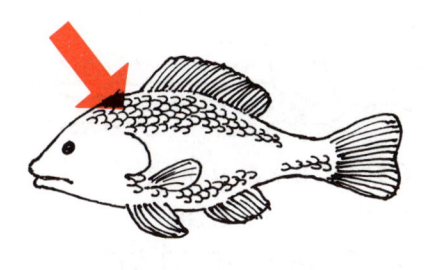

scar a mark left on the skin after a cut has got better
He has a scar on his arm where the dog bit him.

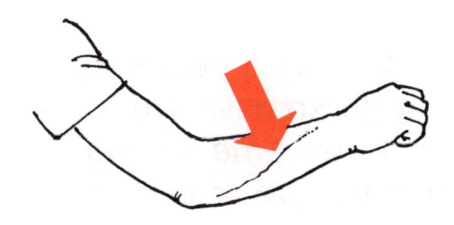

scare frighten
The cat was so scared it ran up a tree.

school the place where you go to learn
My sister is starting school today.

scissors a tool for cutting cloth or paper
Mother used her scissors to cut the cloth.

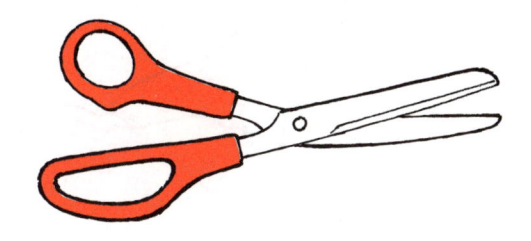

scold speak crossly
The teacher scolded us for making a noise.

scooter a small motor bicycle
When you are on a scooter always wear your helmet.

scrub rub something with a hard brush
I will scrub the kitchen floor. It is very dirty.

sea the salt water that covers most of the earth
You cannot drink sea water.

seal an animal with fur that lives beside the sea.
Seals eat fish.

seat something that you sit on
Father made a seat out of the log.

second 1 a small measure of time
Sixty seconds make one minute.
2 coming after the first
Joe came second in the English test.

secret something that other people must not know about
The money was hidden in a secret place.

see use your eyes
Can you see that aeroplane in the sky?

seed the part of a plant that is put into the ground. A new plant will grow from it
The farmer is sowing his corn seeds.

seem make you think something is true
The cat seems to be asleep. Its eyes are closed.

sell give things to people for money
Mother sells her eggs in the market.

send make a person or thing go somewhere
Please send me a letter when you go to Lusaka.

N n O o P p Q q R r **S s** T t U u V v W w X x Y y Z z

sense seeing, hearing, touching, smelling or tasting
My sense of smell tells me there is a fire in the house.

sensible wise, clever
It is sensible to wear a warm coat when it is cold.

sentence a group of words that make sense
A sentence starts with a large letter and ends with a full stop.

September the ninth month of the year
Father starts his new job in September.

serious 1 very bad
My uncle had a serious car crash.
2 not silly or funny
The teacher is going to have a serious talk with you.

set 1 a group of things that belong together
I will get the set of knives out of the drawer.
2 put or go down
We will be home before the sun sets.

seven the number 7
There are seven days in a week.

seventeen the number 17
My sister is seventeen years old.

seventy the number 70
The bus will hold seventy people.

sew use a needle and thread
Please sew the button on my shirt.

shadow your shape on the ground when you stand in the sun
You can see his shadow when he is standing in front of the light.

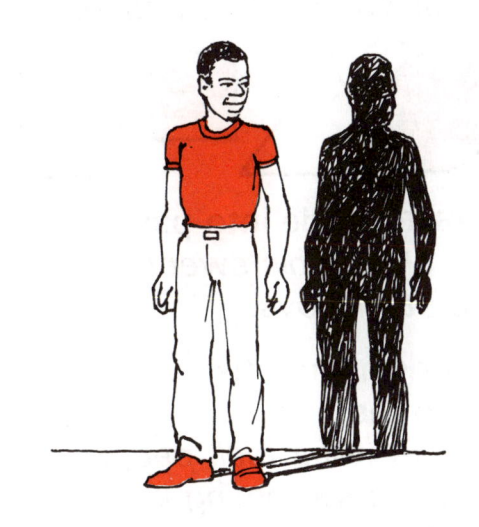

shake move quickly from side to side or up and down
Shake the bottle before you take a drink.

139

A a B b C c D d E e F f G g H h I i J j K k L l M m

shall another word for 'will', going to
I shall leave home at two o'clock.

shallow not deep
You can paddle here. The water is shallow.

shape the way that something looks
A ball has a round shape.

share divide into parts
Jim shared his sweets with the other boys.

shark a large fish with sharp teeth
Sharks will attack people who are swimming in the sea.

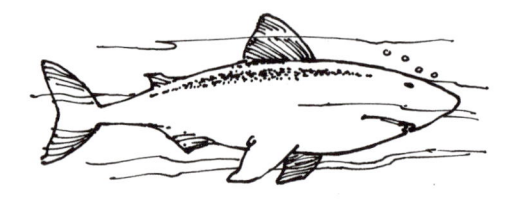

sharp with an edge or point that can cut
The sharp knife cut his finger.

shed a small hut
Father keeps his tools in the shed.

sheep a farm animal, it gives us wool and mutton
A young sheep is called a lamb.

sheet 1 a large piece of cloth that you put on a bed
I have pink sheets on my bed.
2 a piece of paper, glass or metal
Can I have three sheets of paper please?

shelf a long piece of wood fastened to a wall
Put those books back on the shelf.

140

N n O o P p Q q R r **S s** T t U u V v W w X x Y y Z z

shell the hard cover round an egg or a nut or some animals
Snails and some other animals have shells.

shepherd a man who cares for sheep
The shepherd led the flock of sheep up the hill.

shin the front part of the leg between the knee and ankle
My brother hurt his shin playing football.

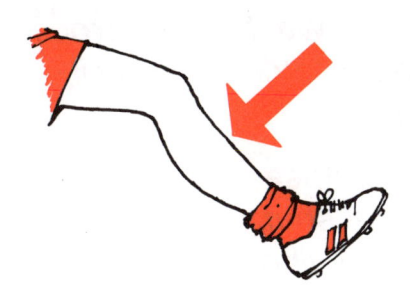

shine give out light
The sun shines during the day.

ship a large boat
A ship can carry many people.

shirt the clothing that is worn on the top half of your body
Sam was wearing a red shirt and a tie.

shiver shake with cold or fear
When the antelope saw the lion it shivered with fright.

shock a surprise that is not nice
We got a shock when we saw that our car was gone.

shoe a strong covering for the foot
I have a pair of red shoes.

shoot fire a gun
Give him the money or he will shoot you.

141

A a B b C c D d E e F f G g H h I i J j K k L l M m

shop a building where people buy things
We have a big grocer's shop in our village.

short not very long
It's a short walk to my house.

shoulder the part of the body between the arm and neck
The men carried the poles on their shoulders.

shout speak loudly
The policeman shouted at the boys to get off the road.

show let someone see something
I am going to show you my new dress.

shower 1 a short fall of rain
The sun will come out soon. It is only a shower.
2 a pipe that sprays water on a person to clean them
I take a shower every morning.

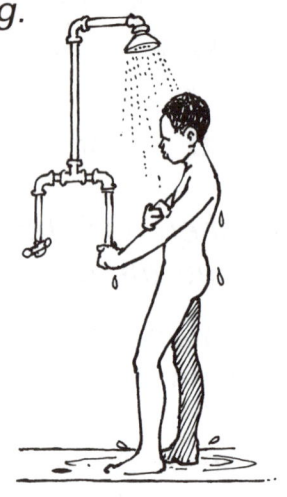

shrink become smaller
Do not wash those trousers in hot water. They will shrink.

shut close
Please shut the gate or the goats will get out.

shy afraid to meet or talk to people
The little girl was shy and hid behind her mother.

sick not well, ill
Mother put me to bed as I was feeling sick.

142

N n O o P p Q q R r **S s** T t U u V v W w X x Y y Z z

side 1 one of the edges of a flat shape, or one of the flat parts of a box
Put that box down on its side.
2 a team that takes part in a sport
Are you playing football for the red side or the green side?

sight 1 to be able to see
The old man is losing his sight.
2 something that is seen
That mountain is a lovely sight.

sign 1 a notice to tell you where to go
Drivers must always follow the road signs.
2 write your name on something
Your mother did not sign this letter.

silent quiet, not talking
The library was silent. There was no noise.

silly not clever
She is a silly girl. She lost her purse.

silver a white metal of great value
She was wearing a beautiful silver brooch.

simple easy
What's two and two? That's a simple question.

since from then until now
I have not seen him since Friday.

sing make a tune with your voice
Please sing one of your lovely songs.

single 1 only one
He has not scored a single goal.
2 not married
She is single, but her brother is married.

sink 1 a large bowl with taps for washing dishes and clothes
My mother washed my shirt in the sink.
2 go down under the water
That ship is going to sink in the storm.

143

A a B b C c D d E e F f G g H h I i J j K k L l M m

sister a girl in a family with other children
My sister is younger than I am. I am her older brother.

sit rest on your bottom
You sit on the chair. I will sit on the bed.

six the number 6
I have six brothers and one sister.

sixteen the number 16
My uncle is coming to see us in sixteen days.

sixty the number 60
There are sixty days in two months.

size how big or small something is
My shoes are size six.

skeleton all the bones in your body

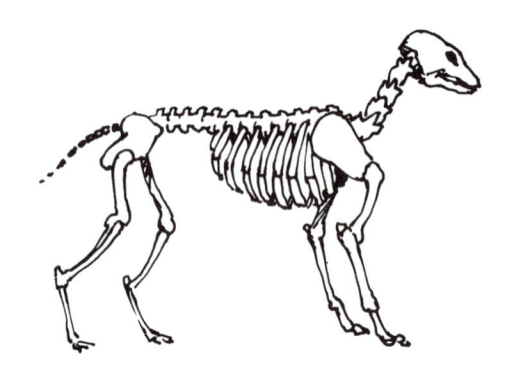

Those bones are the skeleton of a dinosaur.

skin the outside of your body, the outside of some fruit
An apple has a smooth skin.

skip jump over a rope again and again
I love to play and skip with my friends.

skirt girls' clothes, worn from the waist down
The teacher is wearing a long skirt today.

sky all the space around us with the sun, moon and stars
You can see lots of stars in the sky at night.

144

N n O o P p Q q R r **S s** T t U u V v W w X x Y y Z z

slap hit with your hand open
Mother slapped me when I broke the window.

sleep close your eyes and rest
Babies need a lot of sleep.

sleeve a part of a coat or shirt, it covers your arm
He rolled up his sleeves to keep them clean.

slice a piece cut from something
Please give me a slice of that pie.

slide move smoothly over something
The boy slid on the wet grass.

slip nearly fall
The donkey slipped on the wet path up the hill.

slope one side of a hill
We could not ride our bicycles up the steep slope.

slow taking a long time
This train is so slow. We are going to be late.

smack slap
The cruel man smacked the boy on the head many times.

small little, not very big
The puppy was small enough to sleep in a shoe box.

smart neat and tidy
You are wearing a very smart hat.

smash break into many pieces
The jar hit the floor and smashed into pieces.

145

A a B b C c D d E e F f G g H h I i J j K k L l M m

smell use your nose to find something
I can smell the food from here.

smile look happy
The baby smiled when it saw its mother.

smoke the grey gas that comes from a fire
The smoke floated up into the sky.

smooth not rough, level
Glass is smooth.

snail a small animal that lives inside a shell
Snails live inside a shell. They have soft bodies.

snake a long thin animal with no legs
Some snakes are poisonous.

snap break suddenly
The branch snapped in the strong wind.

snatch take something quickly
He snatched my bag and ran away.

sneeze make a sudden noise through your nose
This dust is making me sneeze.

snore breathe noisily when you are sleeping
I hope you don't snore. You will keep me awake all night.

snow small white pieces of frozen ice
Snow falls from the sky when it is very cold.

snug warm and happy
I am snug in my soft bed.

so for that reason
The car would not start so we walked to school.

soak make very wet
That heavy rain will soak your clothes.

soap something that you use with water for washing
I need more soap to finish washing the clothes.

N n O o P p Q q R r **S s** T t U u V v W w X x Y y Z z

sob make a noise when you cry
The little girl sobbed when she burst her ball.

soccer the game of football
There is a soccer match this afternoon.

sock something that you wear on your foot, inside you shoe
Mother told us to put on our shoes and socks.

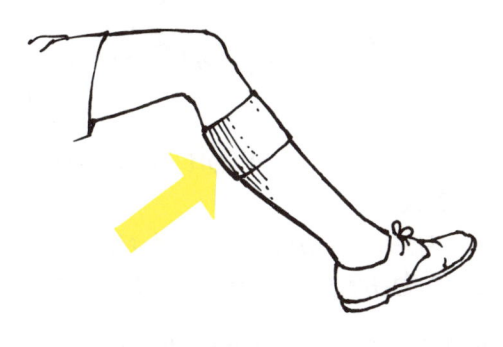

sofa a soft seat for more than one person
Three people can sit on our sofa.

soft not hard
Pillows are soft.

soil the ground that plants grow in
That soil needs a lot of water before we plant the beans.

soldier someone in an army
The soldiers drove the tank across the field.

some a number of things
There are some apples on the table.

someone a person
Someone knocked at the door.

sometimes not all the time
Sometimes I go to school on my bicycle, sometimes I walk.

son a boy child
I have five sons and two daughters.

song words and music for singing
The girls sang a happy song.

soon in a short time from now
The bus will be coming soon.

sore a place on your body that hurts
My legs are sore after playing football.

147

A a B b C c D d E e F f G g H h I i J j K k L l M m

sorry sad about something
My sister dropped the cup. She said she was sorry.

sort type of thing
What sort of car does your father have?

sound anything you can hear
Can you hear the sound of the train coming?

sour tasting like bad milk or lemons
I cannot drink this milk. It is sour.

south a point of the compass
Zambia is south of Zaire.

sow 1 put seeds in the ground
I am going to sow tomatoes and beans this year.
2 a female pig
The sow had fourteen little pigs.

space 1 a place with nothing in it
You can park the car in that empty space.
2 any place outside the earth
There are millions of stars in space.

spade a tool with a long handle for digging
I will dig a deep hole with the spade.

spark a small bit of burning wood
A spark flew out of the fire and burnt a hole in the rug.

speak say something
Mother will speak to father about the holiday.

speed how fast something moves
The police car went down the road at a high speed.

spell 1 use the right letters in a word
Can you spell your name?
2 magic words that make something happen
The witch's spell sent everyone to sleep.

N n O o P p Q q R r **S s** T t U u V v W w X x Y y Z z

spend use money to buy things
How much did you spend on food this week?

spider a small animal like an insect with eight long legs
Most spiders make webs to catch flies.

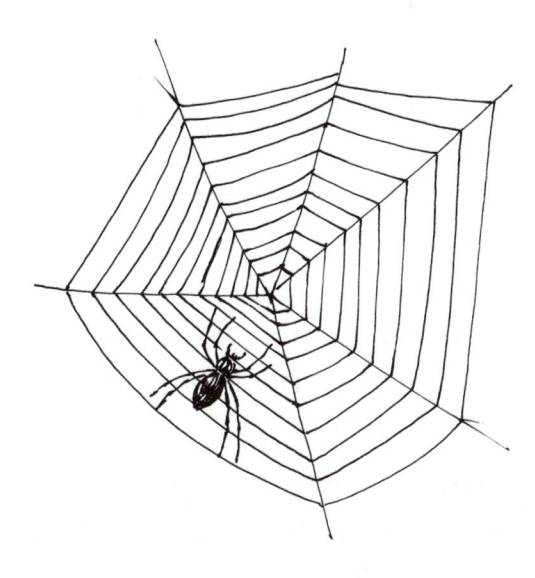

spill let something fall out of a container
Mother spilt the milk on the floor.

spin turn round and round very fast
I was spinning so fast I felt dizzy.

spit shoot liquid out of your mouth
The cat was spitting angrily at the dog.

splash make water fly about
When the boy jumped into the river he splashed us.

split break into parts
The man split the log with his axe.

spoil damage something
Keep your hands clean. You don't want to spoil your dress.

sponge 1 a piece of soft material used for washing
Sponges have a lot of holes in them to soak up water.

2 a soft light cake
I will bake a sponge cake.

A a B b C c D d E e F f G g H h I i J j K k L l M m

spoon something that you use for eating soup or stirring food
Spoons can be made of metal or wood.

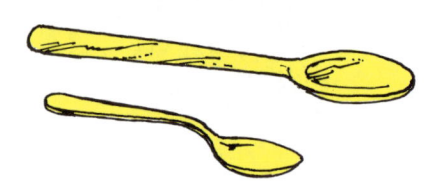

square a shape with four sides the same length
Can you find a square box to put the books in?

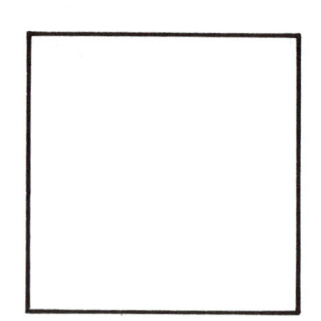

sport a game that you play
Football, netball and tennis are all sports.

spot 1 a small round mark
My sister has a dress with red spots.
    2 see or notice something
The hunter spotted the leopard lying in the grass.

squeak a short high sound
The mouse squeaked when it saw the corn.

squeeze press together
We squeezed the oranges to make juice.

spring 1 a place where water comes out of the ground
Spring water is good to drink.
    2 jump up
The cat sprang up and caught the bird.
    3 the part of the year after winter
New leaves appear on the trees in spring.

150

N n O o P p Q q R r **S s** T t U u V v W w X x Y y Z z

squirrel a small animal that lives in trees
Squirrels have thick furry tails.

stable a building where horses live
There are six horses in the stable.

stain a dirty mark
The ink has left a stain on the cloth.

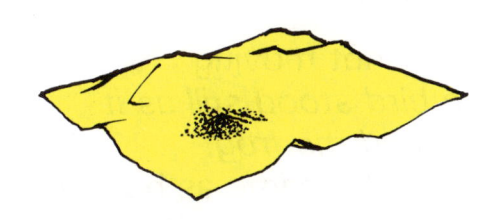

stairs a set of steps inside a building
Go up those stairs to the bedroom.

stamp 1 a small piece of paper with a picture on it
You buy stamps and put them on letters and parcels.
2 bang your foot on the ground
She stamped her foot in anger.

stand 1 stay on your feet
We will stand under the tree until the rain stops.
2 something that you put things on
Put the cake stand in the middle of the table.

star one of the lights you see in the sky at night
The stars look like diamonds in the night sky.

stare look at something for a long time
She stared at the boy who was beating the dog.

start begin
I will start the race when you are all ready.

A a B b C c D d E e F f G g H h I i J j K k L l M m

station 1 a place where buses and trains stop
I will wait for the train at the station.
    2 a place where policemen or firemen work
They took the thief to the police station.

stay be in one place
Father is staying at home tonight.

steal take something that is not yours
That cat is going to steal the fish.

steam the gas that comes from boiling water
Be careful! That steam will burn you.

steep sloping quickly
We cannot climb the hill. It is too steep.

step 1 move your foot when walking or running
Step over the dog or he will bite you.
    2 stairs outside the house
Where do these steps lead to?

stew meat and vegetables cooked in water and gravy
Mother is making stew today.

stick 1 a thin piece of wood
I need some sticks to light the fire.
    2 fix with paste
Will you stick the stamp on the letter?

still 1 not moving
The bird stood still as it watched the frog.
    2 the same as before
Are you still here? You said you were going an hour ago.

sting a part of an animal or plant that can hurt you
A wasp sting is very sore.

152

N n O o P p Q q R r **S** s T t U u V v W w X x Y y Z z

stitch in sewing, to put the thread through the cloth
I am learning to stitch with a needle.

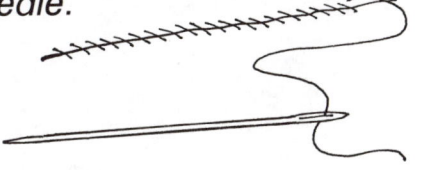

stomach the place in your body where food goes
I ate too much. I have a pain in my stomach.

stone 1 a small piece of rock
Don't throw stones. They can break windows.

2 the hard seed in soft fruit
Never eat the stone in a peach.

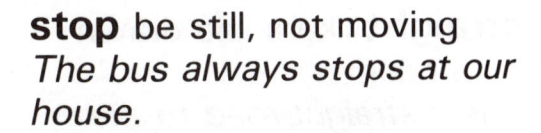

stop be still, not moving
The bus always stops at our house.

store a large shop
Mother buys bread at the food store.

storm a strong wind with a lot of rain
Two houses were damaged in the bad storm.

story true or untrue things someone tells you
Father tells us a story every night.

stove a thing for heating a room or for cooking
The stove makes the room very warm.

153

straight like a line drawn by a ruler
It is a straight road to the village.

stripes wide lines of different colours
Our flag has black stripes.

strange something you do not know or have not seen before
That is a strange bird. What is its name?

stream a small river
Small streams flow into the river.

street a road with houses on each side
We don't live in a street. We live in the country.

stretch pull to make something longer or bigger
That piece of elastic will stretch round the box.

string a very thin rope used for tying things
My sister tied my birthday present with red string.

stroke touch gently with your hand
I like to stroke my kitten.

strong able to lift heavy things
Elephants are very strong. They can lift trees.

student someone who goes to school
My sister is a student at a secondary school.

stupid cannot learn quickly, foolish
He is stupid. He cannot add fifteen and eighteen.

sty a house for pigs
Ten pigs live in that sty.

N n O o P p Q q R r **S s** T t U u V v W w X x Y y Z z

submarine a boat that can go under the water
That submarine went round the world underwater.

subtract take one number away from another number
Subtract four from ten. The answer is six.

10 − 4 = 6

suddenly very quickly
I was walking in the road. Suddenly I saw a car.

sugar the food we put in tea or other food to make it sweet
I don't like tea without sugar.

suitcase a box for carrying clothes
My mother is packing the suitcase. We are going to visit my uncle.

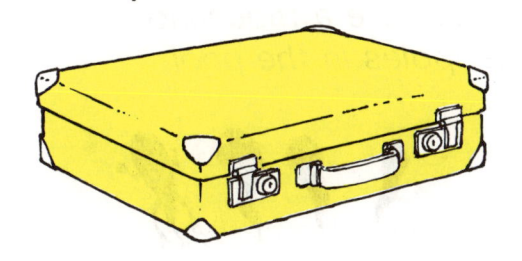

sum a question with numbers
I have five sums to do for school.

summer the hottest part of the year
I like to swim in the river in summer.

sun the bright star that gives us heat and light
There are lots of clouds. You cannot see the sun.

Sunday the first day of the week
I always stay in bed on Sunday morning.

supper a meal you eat in the evening
I like to eat bread and butter for supper.

sure knowing something is true
I'm sure I put the bottle in the box.

surprise when something happens suddenly
My birthday party was a lovely surprise.

A a B b C c D d E e F f G g H h I i J j K k L l M m

swallow 1 put food from your mouth into your stomach
Always chew your food before you swallow it.
2 a bird with a long tail
You can see swallows flying every evening.

swan a big white bird with a long neck
Look! There is a swan and her babies in the river.

sweet 1 taste like sugar
This tea is too sweet. I don't like sugar.
2 a food made from sugar or chocolate
My father says sweets are bad for your teeth.

swim move in the water kicking your arms and legs
The boys are learning to swim in the river. They will be good swimmers.

swing a seat fixed to a branch with ropes
Father made us a swing near the house.

switch something you press to put on the electric light
We have electric switches in every room.

sword a very long, sharp knife for fighting
Soldiers don't use swords today.

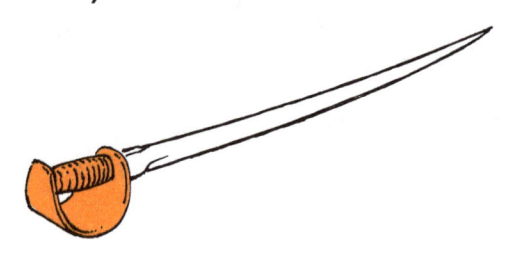

Tt

table a piece of furniture with a flat top for eating and working
I do my sums at the table after school.

tadpole a young frog
There are a thousand tadpoles in the pool.

N n O o P p Q q R r S s **T t** U u V v W w X x Y y Z z

tail the back part of an animal or an aeroplane
Some monkeys have very long tails.

take 1 get hold of something
Take the pen in your hand. Now write with it.
   2 carry away
My sister has taken my sweets.

talk speak to people
Stop talking and get on with your work.

tambourine a round thing like a small drum, you shake or hit it to make music
You shake a tambourine to make music.

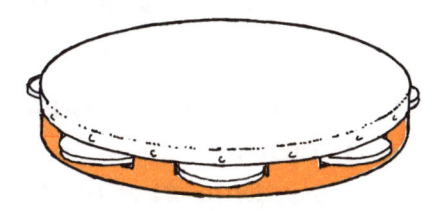

tank 1 a large container for holding liquid
The hot-water tank is leaking.
   2 a heavy vehicle used in war
A tank has a big gun on top.

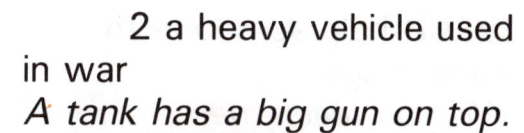

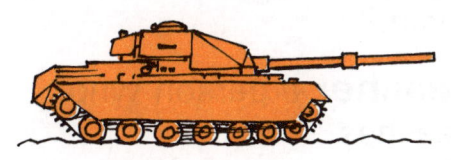

tap 1 a handle to open or close a water pipe
She turned on the tap to fill the sink with water.
   2 hit gently
He tapped on the door before coming in.

tape 1 a narrow piece of material
The teacher fixed the book with tape.
   2 a narrow plastic ribbon used to make music on a machine
Can I borrow your music tape?

taste eat a little bit of food to see if you like it
This soup tastes very good.

taxi a car you pay to travel in
Mother takes a taxi to work every day.

tea a hot drink, you make it with dried leaves
I like a cup of tea with my breakfast.

157

A a B b C c D d E e F f G g H h I i J j K k L l M m

teach help someone to learn things
Will you teach me how to swim?

teacher a person who teaches
The teacher showed us how to do the sums.

team a group of people, they work or play together
I am playing on the netball team.

tear 1 a drop of water, it comes from your eye when you cry
The man gave him a handkerchief to wipe his tears.
2 cut or damage something
Did he tear his trousers on the nail?

telephone a machine that you use to speak to someone who is far away
I will telephone my sister in Lusaka.

television a machine that shows pictures of people and things. The pictures come from far away
We watched the news on the television.

tell say what has happened or is going to happen
Will you please tell me what the man was doing?

temper the way a person feels
I hope father is in a good temper today.

temperature how hot or cold something or someone is
The doctor said I had a very high temperature. He gave me some medicine.

ten the number 10
There are ten oranges left.

tennis a game where you hit a ball with a racket
He wore new white shorts to play tennis.

tent a kind of small house made of cloth
We are sleeping in a tent tonight.

N n O o P p Q q R r S s **T t** U u V v W w X x Y y Z z

term the weeks when you go to school
We have three terms in our school each year.

test questions you have to answer
How did you do in your History test?

than showing the difference between people or things
I am taller than my sister.

thank tell someone you are happy with what he has done or given you
John thanked his uncle for the birthday present.

that the one over there
That is my pen. This is yours over here.

then 1 after that time
First they ate their dinner. Then they had coffee.
　　2 at that time
They were living in Angola then.

there in that place or to that place
I put the three books over there.

thick measuring a lot from one side to the other
The bread was cut in thick slices.

thief a person who steals things
The police caught the thief in our house.

thin not fat
That boy is very thin. Is he ill?

thing anything that can be seen or touched
What is that thing lying in the road?

think 1 use your mind
Think hard before you give your answer.
　　2 have an idea
Do you think I should make this fence higher?

third 1 coming after second
He was the third person to arrive late.
　　2 one of three parts
I want a third of the bar of chocolate.

159

A a B b C c D d E e F f G g H h I i J j K k L l M m

thirsty need a drink
I am very thirsty after that long walk.

thirteen the number 13
There are thirteen nails in the gate.

thirty the number 30
My father is thirty years old.

thousand the number 1 000
There were one thousand people at the football match.

thread a long, thin piece of cotton used for sewing
I sewed on the button with a needle and thread.

three the number 3
I called him three times on the telephone.

throat the front of the neck
Mother has a sore throat.

through from one end to the other
We walked through the forest.

throw make something fly through the air
Can you throw that stone across the river?

thumb the short, thick finger on your hand
Your thumbs help you to hold things.

thunder a loud noise, you hear it during a storm
I hid under the bed when I heard the thunder.

Thursday the fifth day of the week
My brother is going fishing on Thursday.

tick 1 the sound a clock makes
That ticking clock is keeping me awake.
2 a small mark like this √
The teacher ticked my sums to show they were right.
3 a very small insect
A tick bit him. It made him very ill.

ticket a small piece of paper, you buy it to go on the bus or a train or to a football match
I am going to buy a ticket for the match.

tickle touch someone's skin to make him laugh
Please don't tickle my feet.

160

N n O o P p Q q R r S s **T t** U u V v W w X x Y y Z z

tide the rise and fall of the sea
The tide comes in and out twice a day.

tidy have everything neat and clean
I have tidied the kitchen.

tie 1 a thin piece of material worn round the neck
Men wear ties under the collar of their shirts.
2 fasten something with string or rope
The donkey is tied to the tree.

tiger a big, wild animal with stripes
The tiger belongs to the cat family.

till 1 until
Can you wait till my mother comes?
2 a drawer for money in a shop
Always lock the till when you leave the shop.

time 1 seconds, minutes, hours, days, weeks, months, years
This is going to take a long time.
2 one moment of the day
Is it time to go to bed?

tin a round metal container.
I ate a tin of beans

tip 1 the point or end of something
The tip of this pencil is broken.
2 turn upside down
He tipped the rubbish over the floor.

tired need to rest or sleep
The little boy was very tired. He fell asleep on the chair.

toad an animal like a frog
Toads have rough, dry skins and live on the land.

toast bread that is cooked until it is brown
Mother makes toast for breakfast.

A a B b C c D d E e F f G g H h I i J j K k L l M m

today this day
Today we are not going to school.

toe one of the parts at the end of your foot
You have five toes on each foot.

toffee a sweet made from butter and sugar
I bought a bag of toffees in the shop.

together with another person or thing
The two boys walked home together.

toilet a place where you can move old food out of your body
We have a toilet in our house.

tomato a round red vegetable
You can eat raw tomatoes in salad.

tomorrow the day after today
I'm going to school tomorrow. It's Monday.

tongue the long pink part inside your mouth
You talk with your tongue.

too 1 as well
Can I come too?
    2 more than is needed
You have given me too much rice.

tool something that helps you to do a job
Uncle keeps his tools in the tool shed.

tooth one of the hard white things in your mouth
You use your teeth to bite and chew food.

toothpaste something you use to clean your teeth
Put plenty of toothpaste on your brush to clean your teeth.

top the highest part
The goats climbed to the top of the hill.

162

N n O o P p Q q R r S s **T t** U u V v W w X x Y y Z z

torch a small light, you can carry it
You need batteries to make a torch work.

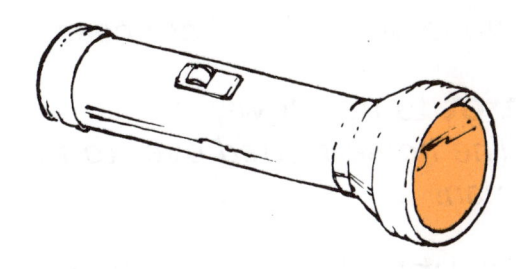

touch feel things
Do not touch that fire, you will burn your hand.

towards moving nearer to someone or something
The baby giraffe ran towards its mother.

towel a piece of cloth for drying things
The man dried himself with a towel.

town a place with many houses and shops where people live
There is a large hospital in our town.

toy something to play with
Can I play with your toys?

track 1 a path
We followed the track down to the river.
2 the marks that people, animals or things make on the ground
The lion tracks in the sand were easy to follow.

traffic the cars, buses and other things that travel on the road
There is a lot of traffic on the road today.

train 1 a number of trucks joined together. An engine pulls them along rails
The train was bringing coal from the mine.
2 teach a person or animal how to do things
He trained the horse to jump fences.

trap something that you catch animals in
The leopard was caught in the trap.

163

A a B b C c D d E e F f G g H h I i J j K k L l M m

travel go on a journey
My uncle has travelled all over the world.

tray a flat piece of wood or metal, we use it to carry food and dishes
I will carry the tray of dishes to the table.

treasure something very valuable
The boys found the treasure buried in the woods.

treat act in a good or a bad way
That man treats his dog very badly. He beats it all the time.

tree a tall plant with leaves and branches
The elephants rested under the tree.

triangle a shape with three straight sides
Draw a triangle in your book, please.

trick make someone believe something that is not true
He tricked me into giving him the money.

trip fall
The girl tripped over the stone and fell on her knees.

trot to run slowly
The horse trotted over to the man.

trouble 1 something that upsets or worries you
Are you in trouble? Can I help you?
2 take great care
She went to a lot of trouble to find this material.

trousers clothing for your legs
Father is wearing his brown trousers today.

truck 1 a cart pulled by a railway engine
The train pulled trucks full of coal.
2 a lorry
The truck made a lot of noise.

true real or correct
Is it true that you are going to another school?

N n O o P p Q q R r S s **T t** U u V v W w X x Y y Z z

trumpet a thing that you blow to make music
My friend plays a trumpet in the school band.

trunk 1 the thick stem of a tree
We will cut the tree trunk up for firewood.
2 a large box to keep clothes in
Mother packed our old clothes in the trunk.

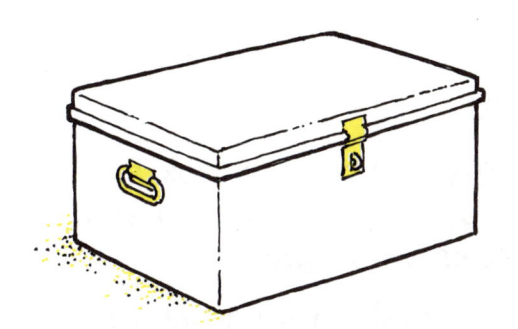

3 an elephant's nose
The elephant pulled down the tree with its trunk.

truth something that is true
You are not telling me the truth. You broke the window.

try work hard to do something
I tried to fix the motor.

tube a long, thin, round object
Where is that tube of toothpaste?

Tuesday the third day of the week
My sister is going to hospital on Tuesday.

tug give a hard pull
He tugged at the weed, but he could not move it.

tune a piece of music
Please play that tune again.

tunnel a long hole under the ground or through a hill
The tunnel was five kilometres long.

turkey a large bird, we often eat them
We need a big oven to cook the turkey in.

turn move round
Push the pedals and the wheels will turn round.

A a B b C c D d E e F f G g H h I i J j K k L l M m

tusk one of an elephant's long pointed teeth
The elephant had a broken tusk.

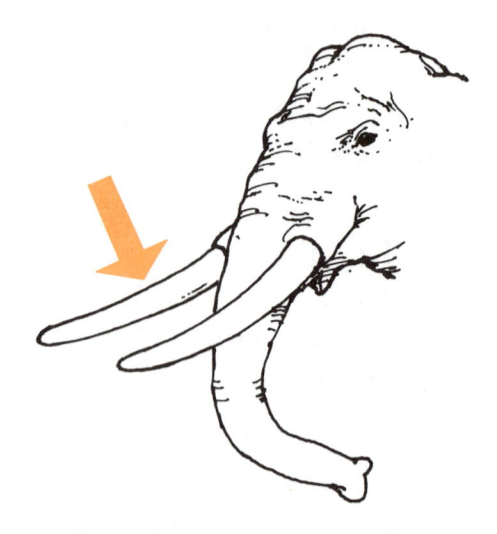

twelve the number 12
There are twelve months in a year.

twenty the number 20
I have twenty books in the house.

twice two times
That is a good book. I read it twice.

twig a thin branch
You can use the twigs to light the fire.

twin one of two children born at the same time to the same mother
One twin is a boy. The other twin is a girl.

two the number 2
A bicycle has two wheels.

type 1 one kind of thing
That type of car goes very fast.
2 write with a machine
She types all her letters on her typewriter.

tyre the rubber tube on a wheel
I have a puncture in the tyre on my bicycle.

Uu

ugly not nice to look at
That is a strange animal. It looks very ugly.

umbrella a round cloth on a stick to stop the rain making you wet
It is raining. Put up your umbrella.

166

N n O o P p Q q R r S s T t **U u** V v W w X x Y y Z z

unable not able to do something
He broke his leg. He is unable to walk.

uncle a brother of your father or mother
I have only one uncle. He is married to my aunt Maria.

under below
Mother is sitting under the tree.

understand know something well
I understand the words in that book.

undo open or untie
Undo the string and open the parcel.

unhappy sad, not happy
She is very unhappy. Her puppy is lost.

uniform the clothes you wear at school or for your job
I always wear my school uniform to school.

unless if you don't
Mother cannot hear you unless you shout.

untidy in a mess
You are very untidy. Your clothes are a mess.

untie open a knot
He untied his laces and took his shoes off.

until up to a certain time
Every night I work until nine o'clock.

upset be sad or cross
My mother is upset. She broke a dish.

upside-down turned over so that the top is at the bottom now
My bicycle is upside-down. I am washing it.

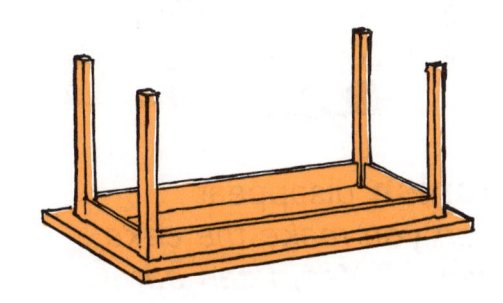

use do a job with something
I use soap and water to wash my bicycle.

useful helps to do a job
That watch is very useful. It tells the time and the date.

usual something that happens often
I am going to school at the usual time today.

A a B b C c D d E e F f G g H h I i J j K k L l M m

Vv

valley low land with hills all around
There is a little valley with a river in the hills.

valuable costs a lot of money
That is a big car. It must be very valuable.

van a small lorry
The man put the parcels into the van.

vanish disappear
Can you make the cake vanish? Yes, I can eat it.

vase a bowl for flowers
Put the flowers in that beautiful vase.

vegetable a plant you can eat
Peas and beans and carrots are vegetables.

vehicle anything that carries people, like cars, vans, buses, bicycles or trains
Which vehicle is taking us to town?

vein a small tube in your body carrying blood
Look! You can see the little blue veins in his hand.

verb a word that tells what someone is doing
The boy hit the goat. 'Hit' is a verb.

verse a part of a poem or a song
I will sing the first verse. You can sing the second verse.

very most
Ice cream is very cold. It is very good on a hot day.

vest the clothes you wear under a shirt
It is very cold. He is wearing a vest and a jersey.

vet a doctor for animals
The vet is coming to give our cows an injection.

N n O o P p Q q R r S s T t U u **V v** W w X x Y y Z z

view all you can see from one place
There is a beautiful view from the top of that hill.

village a small group of houses and shops in the country, a very small town
We live in a village near the river.

vinegar a sour liquid eaten with other food
I eat vinegar with fish and chips.

violet a purple colour
Paint the flowers in your picture violet and red.

violin a thing for playing music
Mother plays the piano. I can play the violin.

visit go to see someone
We visit my uncle in hospital every day.

voice the sound you make when you speak
Keep your voice down. Father is sleeping.

volcano a mountain, flames and rocks come from the top
Look at the fire coming from the volcano!

vowels the letters a, e, i, o, and u
How many vowels are there in the alphabet?

vulture a large bird, it eats dead animals
Look at the vultures. They must see a dead animal.

Ww

wade walk through water
The water is not deep. We can wade out to the boat.

wag move from side to side
The dog is happy. It is wagging its tail.

wagon a cart pulled by horses or oxen
The wagon is carrying four big tree trunks.

169

A a B b C c D d E e F f G g H h I i J j K k L l M m

waist the middle of your body, below your chest
She wore a belt round her waist.

wait stop or stay in one place
John is waiting for the bus at the bus stop.

wake stop sleeping
I wake up when the sun rises.

walk move on your feet
I walk to school every morning.

wall 1 the side of a room
We can put the pictures on the wall.
2 a fence made with stones or bricks
We will build a wall to keep the cows in.

walrus a large sea animal, it likes cold water
The walrus loves to play in the ice.

want wish you can have something
I want some bread and butter.

war a fight between two countries
Many soldiers died in the war.

warm gentle heat
That's a good fire. This room is warm.

was part of the verb 'to be', it tells about the past
I was in school until six o'clock yesterday.

wash clean something with water
My mother washes the clothes in a washing machine.

wasp a large flying insect that stings
There are three wasps eating the jam.

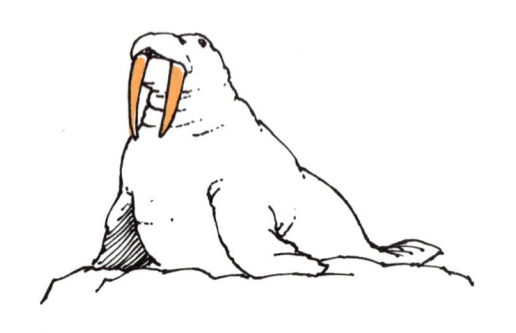

N n O o P p Q q R r S s T t U u V v **W w** X x Y y Z z

watch 1 a small clock, you wear it on your wrist
Have you a watch? What time is it?
2 look at
Watch the snail! It moves very slowly.

water the liquid in rivers and the sea
The boys are swimming in the cold water in the river.

wave move your hand from side to side to say hello or goodbye
There is your aunt. Wave your hand.

way 1 a road
Take that road. That's the way to the village.
2 how to do something
Watch me. You kick a ball this way.

wax a white material, we make candles with it
We can buy candles to see in the dark.

weak not very strong
The old man is too weak to lift the heavy box.

wear have clothes on
I am wearing a green dress today.

weather the rain, sunshine or wind we get during the day
I hope there will be sunny weather today.

web a thin net, a spider makes it
There were two flies in the spider's web.

wedding the time when two people are married
My sister is married now. I went to her wedding.

Wednesday the fourth day of the week
We always do sport on Wednesday.

weed a wild plant
There are more weeds than flowers in the garden.

week seven days
My father works five days a week, from Monday to Friday.

weigh how heavy something is
My sister is tall, but I weigh more than she does.

welcome be happy to see someone
My friend's mother welcomed me to her house.

171

A a B b C c D d E e F f G g H h I i J j K k L l M m

well 1 be in good health
I was ill, but I am well now.
2 a hole in the ground, we get water from it
We get lots of water from the well.

were the same as 'was' but talking about two or more people
I was happy. They were very unhappy.

west the direction where the sun sets
Our village is to the west of the city.

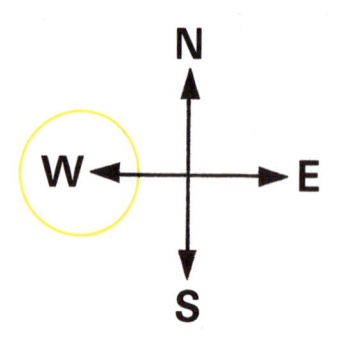

wet covered with water
It is raining. I am very wet.

whale a very large sea animal
Whales are the biggest animals in the world.

what asking a question about a person or a thing
What time is it? What are you doing?

wheat a plant, its seeds give us flour for bread
The farmer is cutting the field of wheat.

wheel the big round parts of a bicycle or a car, they turn to move it
Bicycles have two wheels. Cars have four.

when 1 at this time
We are going to the party when I finish my work.
2 asking a question, at what time?
When are you going to the party?

where what place?
Where are you going? I'm going to school.

which asking you to choose a person or thing
Which skirt do you want?

while at the same time
While you work, I will read my book.

172

N n O o P p Q q R r S s T t U u V v **W w** X x Y y Z z

whisper speak very quietly
Don't tell mother. Whisper to me.

whistle 1 make a sound with your lips
Can you whistle a song for me?
2 a thing for making this sound
I have a whistle for the soccer referee to blow.

white the colour of milk
Swans are white birds.

who asking a question about a person
Who is that man in the shop?

whole all of something
I ate the whole cake.

why asking the reason
Why did you take the book? It is mine.

wide far from one side to the other
This is a very wide road. Four cars can drive on it.

wife a married woman
John and his wife have two children.

wild living in nature, not looked after by people
The forest is full of wild animals.

will a word to say you are going to do something
I will come to see you tomorrow.

willing happy to do something
He is always willing to help his mother.

win come first in a game
He is very good at running. He will win the race.

wind the air moving quickly
The wind was very strong. It blew the tree down.

window a hole in a wall covered with glass
Look out the window. You can see the rain.

windscreen the glass in the front window of a car
The boy threw a stone. It broke the windscreen.

173

A a B b C c D d E e F f G g H h I i J j K k L l M m

wing a part of a bird, an insect or aeroplane
Birds use their wings to fly.

wink close and open one eye quickly
When you want me to stop, wink.

winter the coldest part of the year, it comes after the autumn
We wear warm clothes in winter.

wipe clean with a cloth
The window is dirty. Wipe it with a clean cloth.

wire a thin metal thread
My father uses wire to make a fence.

wise knowing a lot of things
My uncle is very wise. He helps me a lot.

wish ask for something to happen
I wish I had a lot of money.

witch a woman who can do magic
My sister says the old lady is a witch.

with having something
I ride a bicycle with red wheels.

without not having
He went home without his school books.

wizard a man who can do magic
Mother says wizards can do magic.

wolf a large, grey animal like a wild dog
Listen! That is a wolf howling.

woman a grown-up female
That woman is my aunt.

wonderful very good
We went to the city yesterday. It was a wonderful day.

wood 1 a lot of trees
They are cutting down some of the trees in the wood.
2 what trees are made of
The tables and chairs are made of wood.

wool the thick hair of a sheep
The sheep look warm with their thick wool.

word a group of letters that make sense
Look at the words in that book.

174

N n O o P p Q q R r S s T t U u V v **W w** X x Y y Z z

work do a job
My mother works in a bank.

world the earth and everything on it
I want to fly round the world.

worm a long, thin animal, it lives in the soil
The worm is wriggling about in the earth.

worse not so good
He is a worse swimmer than I am.

worst very bad
He is the worst swimmer in the class.

wrap put paper round, make into a parcel
Wrap up the present in the red paper.

wreck a badly damaged car or building
That car is a wreck. Was the driver hurt?

wriggle bend and turn like a worm
The girl wriggled through the hole in the hedge.

wrist a part of your arm, it joins your arm to your hand
He looked at the watch on his wrist.

write put words down on paper
I am going to write a letter to my brother.

wrong not right, not correct
That is the wrong way to do the sum.

Xx

x-ray a picture that shows the inside of the body
You go to a hospital to get an x-ray.

Yy

yacht a boat with sails
The yachts raced across the lake.

175

A a B b C c D d E e F f G g H h I i J j K k L l M m

yard a piece of ground with a wall round it
The farmer put his cattle in the yard.

yawn open your mouth wide and breathe in, you do it when you are tired
He was so tired after work that he could not stop yawning.

year twelve months
We have been living in this house for one year.

yeast a brown powder, bakers make bread with it
My mother puts yeast in the flour to make bread.

yell shout loudly
The man yelled at the boy to stay away from the fire.

yellow the colour of butter
The bananas are ripe. They are yellow.

yesterday the day before today
Mother did her washing yesterday.

yet until now
I haven't done my homework yet.

yolk the yellow part of an egg
The yolk is the nicest part of the egg.

young not old, born a short time ago
He is too young to eat a banana.

youth the time when you are young
She was a good swimmer in her youth.

Zz

zebra an animal like a horse with stripes
A zebra has black and white stripes.

zero the number 0
His work was so bad the teacher gave him a zero.

zigzag a line with very sharp turns
Look! The road zigzags up the mountain.

zip a long metal fastener
Please zip up my dress.

zoo a place to keep wild animals
We are going to the zoo tomorrow.